shed chic

Country Living
MAGAZINE

shed chic

sally coulthard

jacqui
small

First published in 2009 by Jacqui Small LLP
An imprint of Aurum Press Ltd
7 Greenland Street
London NW1 OND

Publisher **Jacqui Small**
Commissioning Editor **Joanna Copestick**
Art Director **Gabriella Le Grazie**
Managing Editor **Lesley Felce**
Picture and Location Research **Nadine Bazar**
 and **Sarah Airey**
Production **Peter Colley**

ISBN 978 1 906417 18 5

A catalogue record for this book is available from
the British Library.

2011 2010 2009

10 9 8 7 6 5 4 3 2 1

Printed in China

CONTENTS

CONTENTS

introduction

There is something irresistibly comforting and immensely appealing about the shed. For generations, these modest garden buildings were considered the last male bastion, a retreat from work and wife, and a place to potter. But times have changed. Life at the bottom of the garden has become infinitely more interesting. We buy more sheds than ever, in all shapes and sizes. We use them for every imaginable purpose, from craft workshop to children's playhouse, guest annexe to garden room, and they are no longer solely a male domain.

For an increasing number of people, it seems as if sheds have become the perfect solution to the demands of modern life. As designer Sir Terence Conran once noted, a shed's enduring appeal is its separateness – where else can you escape from the house without travelling more than a few metres? Your shed might be only a minute down the garden path, but it is a million miles away from the noise and distractions of daily life.

What better place to relax and recharge your batteries when required?

Equally, many people who work from home find that the only place they can concentrate is away from the main house. It can be difficult to focus when your attention is diverted by chores or noisy offspring. A shed home office is the ideal solution – all the professionalism of an office without the daily commute. And, thanks to advances in technology such as broadband and WiFi, there's no reason your shed cannot be as well connected as any city-based firm.

At the same time, a shed's very proximity to your property is another point in its favour. We may all dream of a romantic retreat or a distant place of solitude, but, from the point of view of security, it is good to know that you can keep an eye on your shed at all times. And that you can pop back and forth when the mood strikes.

From their humble origins as places of shelter and storage (the word 'shed' is a

OPPOSITE A gardener's retreat: the classic hallmark of a British country garden. ABOVE RIGHT Work from home, relax in the garden or simply transport yourself to another place. Sheds have many uses.

derivation of 'shade'), sheds are now considered an attractive addition to the home. The combination of high house prices and the demand for more room has encouraged many of us to look to the outside for more living space. Extensions, lofts and basement conversions are expensive options, and not always viable. They can also be very disruptive. Building a shed, on the other hand, tends to be cheaper and faster to construct, and involves a minimum of disruption to your existing house.

Sheds are also eminently portable. Most sheds come in kit form and can easily be dismantled and rebuilt on a new site – perfect if you ever decide to move home. Some manufacturers of the more expensive sheds even offer a relocation service; if you tell them you plan to move the shed at some stage, they can reinforce the structure so that it can be removed from your garden by crane, and taken to your new nest at a later stage. Indeed, this gives you the flexible option of being able to transform your shed into a movable outdoor building all year round.

The planning process for sheds can be a simple one, depending on the individual shed's sophistication and its intended use. Some sheds are classed as portable buildings and, as such, are not subject to such stringent planning laws as permanent buildings. But check with your local planning authority first. Rules and regulations about height, size and location, as well as other factors, may well apply.

Although sheds are simple structures, they can still be warm and welcoming. Heating, electricity and water are relatively easy to connect to your shed, making it almost entirely self-contained, while adequate

LEFT Forget the disorganized clutter of lawn mowers and garden tools. Make your shed a home from home. OPPOSITE Need room to breathe? Sheds can add much-needed living space to your home, as well as potentially increase its value.

LEFT Even the simplest of shelters can become a heavenly hideaway. RIGHT This simple hut occupies a prime position at the bottom of a garden, screened by shrubs and overlooking a pond.

insulation and comfortable furniture can turn even the most basic of boxes into a cosy hideaway. And there are endless types of sheds from which to choose – from simple larch-lap potting sheds to architect-designed beach huts. This book covers the myriad of uses people put their sheds to – from reading rooms to summerhouses. Sheds suit many locations, from lakeside to backyard, cottage garden to coast.

Whether you build a home office or a shepherd's hut, you should easily recoup your costs and add kerbside appeal to your home. By stashing away all the tools, bikes and other equipment that usually clog up the outside space, you will instantly create a neater garden.

A shed can hugely improve your enjoyment of your property. By expanding your available living space, you will feel less crowded in your home; you may also be able to enjoy hobbies or pursuits that you were previously unable to accommodate indoors, amongst your daily living space. Whether it's a stained-glass workshop or a photographic darkroom, a shed can be an ideal creative space, especially for those activities which are too noisy or messy for your main home.

Whatever your motive for wanting a shed, this book aims to guide you through the practical considerations, such as planning and building your outdoor structure, while also giving you inspiration for the kinds of exciting spaces you can design.

SHED DESIGN

Sheds are no longer merely places where old electrical appliances go to die and nothing ever happens. Forget rusty tools and broken deck chairs – today's sheds are more likely to house a laptop than a lawn mower. From art studios to saunas, there is a shed to suit all members of the family, giving everyone space and freedom to play, whatever their age or inclination. And, whether you favour traditional country chic or contemporary style, an eco ethos or reclaimed materials, the design possibilities are endless.

LEFT Sheds can range in complexity and design from simple tiny wooden cabins to impressive mini-modernist dwellings.

design choices

Whether you want a shed to echo the design of your home or you wish to create a focal point in the garden, there are many types of buildings to consider.

ABOVE RIGHT Rambling roses and dense planting create the perfect natural backdrop for a country-style shed.
OPPOSITE Weatherboard painted in muted shades, teamed with floral fabrics and a favourite armchair, brings a nostalgic touch to this traditional summer house.

COUNTRY SHEDS

What do you think of when you imagine a rural retreat? Cosy log fires, rustic cottages, breathtaking views, wildlife on your doorstep, clear starry skies and, of course, bags and bags of fresh air. While most of us cannot afford to give up the day job to escape to a rural idyll, you can create a corner of the countryside in your own back garden. A country-style shed is the perfect getaway from the stresses and strains of urban life, and a pretty addition to any garden, whether it is an urban setting or out of town.

How you go about creating this setting is up to you; you can make your shed the star of the show – giving it centre stage in the garden – or you may prefer to blend it into its surroundings, creating a secret hideaway. Traditionally, country sheds are tucked away in the corner of an orchard or knee-deep in a meadow, but they can work equally well in a quiet corner of a suburban lawn.

The most successful country sheds are often made from weatherboarding or cedarwood strips, left plain or painted in creams and natural hues, or perhaps decorated in heritage greens and blues.

Think about the way your shed blends into the planting of your existing plot. Country sheds look great with rambling plants such as climbing roses and lavender growing up the outside. Herbs work well too – mint and spearmint will grow happily around your shed, while chives and other alliums have the added bonus of pretty pink and purple flowers. Any plants in close proximity to the entrance of your shed will have to be able to withstand the occasional knock. Go for robust species such as thyme, oregano, sage, lemon balm, buddleia or rosemary, which are attractive as well as sweet-smelling when you brush past them.

On the exterior, small touches such as window boxes, shutters and weather vanes all add a certain rural appeal, as do patinated

interiors or a coastal New England look, stick with pale cream or white walls woodwork and walls. Country chic mixes nostalgic, whimsical and practical elements to create a relaxed, handcrafted feel. Don't worry about everything being 'perfect' – rustic interiors work best when spontaneous and personal.

Makeshift storage solutions include vintage suitcases, wooden trunks and old tea chests, salvaged school coat hooks and reclaimed shelves. Or make your own informal shelving using an assortment of old bricks and distressed planks of wood.

Spend time browsing the Internet or looking at books and magazines for country-chic inspiration. Interior designers often use a 'mood board' to visualize the finished look. Almost anything can be included – paint samples, fabric swatches, photographs, magazine clippings, sketches – to provide you with inspiration and help you to get some sense of the overall design and decorative scheme. Plot out your best ideas on graph paper for a sense of scale.

OPPOSITE In this basic but beautiful hut, bare wood, a corrugated tin roof and a bold blue door create a functional but appealing shed. ABOVE A pastoral idyll, this painted shed is simply decorated with vintage tools, a wreath on the door and a collection of painted nesting boxes for local birdlife. BELOW A rural-style retreat at the bottom of the garden is a home from home – a perfect solution to the demands of modern life.

metal candle holders or vintage lanterns. Inside, fabrics are a quick way to add rustic charm – gingham, vintage florals and ticking are country-style classics, along with warm woollen blankets and cosy throws. Think about flooring – wide timber floorboards look fantastic, especially whitewashed or waxed – and team it with painted wooden furniture, patchwork cushions, *objets trouvés* such as antique tools, painted nesting boxes for birds, or framed images of old garden roses or even discarded seed packets.

If you want a cluttered, 'cosy cottage' feel, opt for chairs covered with battered leather or floral fabrics, and floral wallpapers or dark-painted tongue-and-groove panelling offset with wall-mounted lights or candle holders. If you prefer light, airy Scandinavian

LEFT Painted tongue-and-groove panelling inside and out is pretty, practical and utterly timeless.
BELOW Stately home chic: a dramatic roofline and turned finial at its peak add a refined touch to this secluded garden folly.
OPPOSITE Ornate bargeboards provide a quirky architectural note on this traditional studio summer house.

(which can be moved through 360 degrees to catch the sun's rays) are especially popular, but antique potting sheds, chalets, playhouses and gypsy caravans are also highly sought after. As with most antiques, condition is everything; a good example can cost thousands, especially if it is made by a well-known manufacturer. Rare sheds tend to come up at specialist auctions, alongside other collectable garden antiques. The larger auction houses, such as Christie's and Sotheby's, will have details of any upcoming sales near you; if not, they should still be able to direct you to a specialist dealer.

TRADITIONAL SHEDS

Many of the most elegant sheds are reproductions of traditional designs – the best are those that faithfully replicate the quality of craftsmanship and materials of their era. If you own a period or listed building, a traditional shed can complement your property beautifully, especially if you try to incorporate some of your home's architectural features into the shed. Can you match the style of windows, for example, or any decorative details from the exterior woodwork? Perhaps you could carry any external paint colours across to the shed.

There is also a small, fiercely competitive market for traditional antique sheds. Most date from the beginning of the twentieth century, as many of the wooden structures built before this time have long since deteriorated. Revolving summer houses

Above Wood in its most natural state – unfinished, untreated and totally unspoilt - is perfectly offset by the surrounding greenery.
Opposite Raw timber strips or logs, left unfinished rather than sawn into smooth planks, give a log cabin its distinctive appearance.

LOG CABINS

When we think of log cabins, we tend to think of North America. When early European settlers first arrived on these shores, they brought with them the ancient craft of log building, a simple type of construction perfectly suited to a timber-rich environment.

Settlers from different parts of the northern hemisphere brought subtly different ways of building the log cabins – the French settlers used square-cut logs, for example – but it was the Scandinavian method of using round logs with bottom-cut corner notches that survived as the characteristic log cabin we recognize today.

Log cabins are still widely used as homes. On a small scale, they also make practical animal shelters and storage spaces, as well as snug and cheerful garden buildings. And no wonder. They are the original eco shed. If made using sustainably sourced timber, log cabins are one of the most environmentally friendly buildings you can buy. They are simple to construct, healthy to live in, and totally biodegradable. They are also naturally cool in summer and warm in winter.

Natural materials and simple colours in earth and forest tones work best for the interior of a log cabin. Many people choose to follow the chalet-chic approach – woollen throws and rugs, roaring log fires, solid wood furniture, cowhide and wildlife memorabilia. This may be, in part, down to the practicalities of living in a rustic building, but there is also an element of creating a 'lifestyle look' reminiscent of those first intrepid settlers. You can direct the look towards traditional hunting lodge or ski-lodge contemporary. Both work.

CONTEMPORARY SHEDS

Contemporary sheds come in all shapes and sizes. They utilize the widest range of materials – metals, glass, plastic, timber, concrete and natural stone – and often in unexpected ways. Uninhibited by tradition, modern sheds break the mould of what we expect when we think of garden buildings. Rather than making do with sitting in a draughty old shack, you can construct a newly designed garden building to suit your personal requirements exactly. You can change the layout to suit your occupation or hobby, and include modern comforts such as air conditioning, underfloor heating, surround sound or ambient lighting. If you run an office from home, a contemporary shed can also easily include all the latest communications and computer devices.

Many specialist companies that design and build contemporary sheds have a strong eco ethos and use only building materials from sustainable sources, especially wood that is certified by the FSC (Forest Stewardship Council). This organization verifies the provenance of wood to ensure that it has not been sourced from irreplaceable rainforests, for instance, and that it has been grown, managed and harvested according to FSC guidelines. Additionally, many contemporary designers ensure that environmental elements such as solar panels, water butts and flower boxes for growing your own produce are included as standard. Indeed, planning authorities may look very kindly on any outdoor buildings that take an environmentally sound approach to design, and therefore be more likely to approve the construction of any larger or more adventurous sheds on this basis.

Contemporary sheds allow us to indulge our design fantasies in a way that our houses never can. Planning laws, rightly, can prevent us from making bold architectural statements with our main homes, but that doesn't mean our sheds have to be dull too. Thanks to the more relaxed approach that planners take towards temporary structures, sheds can be much more adventurous in their construction and appearance. Want a glazed roof? Have one. Fancy a wall made entirely of sheet metal? Why not. Contrary to popular belief, contemporary modern architecture doesn't have to mean that everything is pared down and sterile – it just means that it all serves a specific function.

Thanks to the flexibility and durability of modern materials, many contemporary sheds can be constructed or moved in a matter of days. Many of the modular garden buildings we see today are constructed off-site at the factory, then quickly assembled in your garden, reducing the disruption and chaos of a traditional building project. But it is not just about practicalities. You can have fun with the design of a contemporary shed. About as far removed from the traditional potting shed as you can get, modern garden buildings are light-filled, airy and bright. Energy-efficient, self-cleaning and reflective glass allows you to replace large expanses of walls and roofing with glazing, letting light flood in and creating wonderful working and living spaces. Wood, that most natural of all building materials, is often used in contemporary design. Hardwoods such as cedar and ash are tough, smart and durable, while sturdy but simple decking at the entrance and around the edges of a modern shed is both practical and clean-lined. Indoors, the decor can be taken in any direction, be it minimalist, retro or eco.

Contemporary and period structures can often sit together beautifully and may provide a good foil for each other, so never feel restricted by the age or architectural style of your property. If you live in an historically significant building, there is a good chance that you will be restrained from incorporating über-modern design elements into your home. Bringing a contemporary touch to an old building, in the form of a modern garden building, is a lovely compromise that respects the historical and architectural integrity of the original building, yet gives you something stylish and exciting, new and comfortable, with which to live. A brand-new shed in a period setting provides an element of surprise in the same way that a contemporary, glass-filled extension can make an interesting addition to a traditional house.

BELOW Extensive window glazing will give you a light-filled living or work space and a great view onto the garden.
OPPOSITE TOP Large expanses of reflective glass replace conventional timber in this sleek shed where walls and greenery merge into one.
OPPOSITE BOTTOM LEFT Who said that a shed had to be twee? Daring colours and ultra-modern styling work equally well.
OPPOSITE BOTTOM RIGHT Somewhere to sit: a large pergola provides welcome shade and makes a dramatic design statement.

While many sheds can be bought off-the-shelf, you may want to call in an architect to create something more individual. Architects fulfil a number of important roles in the building process, from initial design drawings to total project management.

When it comes to sheds, it might seem like an extravagance to hire an architect for such a relatively small structure, but it all depends on your budget. Many of the top-end garden buildings can cost as much as a house extension, so it is important that you get the most from your money. Employing an architect means that you will end up with a professionally designed building that has had its overall potential fully and thoughtfully explored during the planning process.

Just bear in mind two things. First, think carefully about why you need an architect. Do you simply need architectural drawings of a shed, or do you want someone to design and project-manage the entire process? Secondly, remember to choose an architect who shares your creative vision. Discuss ideas and images with them, to make sure that you are compatible.

ECO-CHIC SHEDS

When thinking about eco-sheds, many of us imagine a poorly cobbled together building made of recycled materials. Well, think again. Modern eco-sheds are sleek, savvy constructions. Not only are they great to look at, but also part of their elegance comes from the way they function – there is an inherent beauty in a building that works in harmony with its surroundings. But that is not the only benefit. By following green guidelines, the costs of building and running an eco-shed are, over the long term, often less than that of a conventional building.

Modern eco-sheds, designed along clean lines with functional but environmentally friendly utilities such as wood-burning stoves, water butts and natural integral insulation are increasingly popular, in all sorts of settings, both rural and urban.

Timber is the obvious choice for the exterior of an eco-shed, but you will need to ensure that it is ethically sourced. In some parts of the world, shed and fence timber is often grown and felled illegally,

OPPOSITE This modern eco-shed is environmentally sound and effortlessly chic. ABOVE Sustainable timber, recycled materials and low-impact living are all key elements of a green getaway place.

Many contemporary sheds include eco-friendly elements as a matter of course. Think about using some of these features for your shed. Solar panels can help to provide hot water, while a wood-burning stove is an efficient way to keep toasty in the colder months. A grey-water recycling system can be used for the toilet, while water-saving devices are easy to include in any standard bathroom and kitchen. Even a simple water butt attached to the downpipe can collect rainwater for use in and around the garden.

If you want to take the eco-friendly theme further, a sedum roof will provide colour and interest all year round, as well as offering excellent insulation; a living roof will help to keep the shed warm in winter and cool in summer. If you want to disguise your shed for any reason, sedum roofs are also a fantastic way to soften the effect of a shed, helping it to blend into its surroundings and expand the amount of green space on view. Living roofs work particularly well on sheds in urban spaces – they are a great way of replacing the precious amount of green space that is lost when you build a shed in your garden. The only downside of sedum roofs is that they can be heavy, especially when wet; you will need to make sure that the shed frame can hold the extra weight.

If you are serious about designing a substantial eco-shed, it is important to get the basics right. A number of factors affect how 'green' a building is, so take the time to resolve some of the following ecological issues in your project.

The first consideration should be energy use. To be truly environmentally friendly, your

LEFT Clever lighting makes this shed as dramatic by night as it is during the day. OPPOSITE Think about the interplay between a shed and its surroundings. Here, the clean-lined buildings reflect the chic, elegant minimalism of the garden.

shed will have to use significantly less energy than a conventional building. Energy-efficient heating systems and high-performance insulation are two essential factors to include. It is also worth thinking about where your energy comes from – if creating your own renewable energy is an option, then great. But if that is not feasible, consider changing your electricity source to a green supplier to help matters. To complete the energy circle, make sure that you recycle. An eco-shed should have recycling systems as an inherent part of its design, including for any water, paper, plant materials, glass, metals and plastic that you use in its day-to-day function.

How does your garden building sit in relation to its environment? An eco-shed should be sympathetic with its surroundings. Look at the vernacular architecture of the area. Are the building materials in keeping with what is already there? Locally sourcing your building materials not only benefits the local economy, but also cuts your shed's carbon footprint. Make sure that glass is environmentally produced and strongly glazed. How atmospherically destructive will the shed's construction be? Try to keep the environmental impact – felling trees,

for example, to create space for your building project, or using less environmentally sound materials such as concrete for foundations – as minimal as possible. Use recycled materials wherever possible.

How you use the building also has an effect on the environment. An eco-shed should maximize daylight and use low-energy lighting for evenings – does the building make the most of natural daylight and the movement of the sun? As well as considering lighting, factor in the eco-friendliness of other gadgets and appliances in your shed, such as computers or TVs. Do they have an A rating for energy efficiency?

And what about decorating your shed? Most conventional paints contain volatile organic compounds (VOCs) and other toxins, while many timber stains and preservatives pose a particular problem for allergy sufferers. The production of paint is also very energy-intensive. Using eco-paints made from raw materials and natural pigments makes for healthier building and can help to reduce your carbon footprint. Maintenance is also a part of being eco-friendly. Looking after your shed and taking care to make repairs when necessary will extend its life and prevent materials being unnecessarily wasted.

SMALL SHEDS

If either garden space or your budget is limited, think about a small or second-hand shed. Most large DIY stores have an excellent range of outbuildings, including garden tidies and mini-sheds. Off-the-shelf sheds can soon be spruced up with a lick of paint and some personal touches, but, if you want to buy something with a bit more character, many reclamation yards have antique timber garden structures in need of a good home, especially if you are looking to take on a restoration project. Websites can also be helpful in listing suppliers of architectural salvage, including sheds and garden buildings, in your local area.

Modern second-hand sheds are also a real bargain. Look through the pages of any local newspaper with ad listings, and you are bound to find a good selection of sheds on offer, often at a fraction of their original price. Auction websites such as eBay are also a good bet, especially if you can collect the item yourself. You will need to check whether the price of the shed includes dismantling, and be absolutely scrupulous in checking the shed for signs of rot or instability. The roof covering may need replacing, but this is an inexpensive and simple job, as is the replacement of any missing bolts, screws and other fixings. You may even get lucky and pick up a free shed at one of the many Freecycle groups around the globe (see Sources Directory, page 200).

OPPOSITE Size isn't everything. Sometimes the smallest sheds are the most practical.
ABOVE Even a small, secluded shed will give your garden a boost. Stash away all the clutter, and you'll instantly make the garden seem bigger.
RIGHT This diminutive designer shed is perfectly formed and provides just the right amount of necessary storage.

RIGHT Hiding away from the cares of the world – in a fisherman's hut on stilts.
FAR RIGHT Al fresco entertaining with expansive waterside views.
BELOW LEFT Lakeside luxury: making the most of views from a spectacular shoreline.
OPPOSITE A contemporary and ambitious take on the traditional seaside beach hut.

WATERSIDE LIVING

The idea of having a waterside shed holds a special appeal. Whether it is a lakeside cabin or a seaside hut, a bolt hole by the beach or a fishing cabin in the mountains, these kinds of sheds make a perfect place to retire to, away from the hustle and bustle of everyday life, with views that are simply inspiring.

Few of us live by the sea permanently, so a waterside retreat is guaranteed to make any trip feel like a holiday. It also means that these types of sheds tend to be in great demand, with some of the best spots commanding high prices and long waiting lists. If you want to find a place by the sea, regional tourist offices should have details on where and when beach huts are available for rent, or local estate agents may know of huts and houseboats coming up for sale. Local authorities or sometimes private estates may be responsible for the long-term leasing of beach huts, so it is always worth a quick call to your local authority to find out more information about beach-hut hire.

If you are lucky enough to have the land, why not create your own waterside retreat at home. A hut overlooking a favourite pond can be a real treat and an ideal spot from which to watch wildlife. Fallen leaves can choke a pond, so position your pond in a sunny, tree-free part of the garden. If you plant a mixture of oxygenating, floating, emergent and marginal plants, you should attract a good mixture of animal and insect visitors and keep your pond in balance. Your pond could also include a water feature – not only will it oxygenate the water, but running water also adds an extra dimension to any waterside retreat, bringing life, movement and sound to the space.

Don't forget safety issues. Ponds, sheds and young children are not a good combination. Under-fives are the biggest safety risk for drowning, so it is by far the most sensible option to wait until your children are older before installing an unfenced waterside retreat in your back garden. Once you do have a pond, minimize the risks by positioning the pond and its shed where they can both be easily seen from the house, designing the pond with gently sloping edges, and installing a safety grid just underneath the water's surface in case any mishaps do occur. Once appropriate safety measures are in place, everyone can sit back, relax and enjoy the peaceful setting.

ON THE MOVE

The ultimate means by which to perform a romantic escape from everyday life is to decorate and furnish your very own shed on wheels, creating a mobile home-from-home that is innately appealing as a stand-alone structure. In addition, these traditional vehicles are cute and compact inside, with space-saving features and decorative details.

Such appealing wagons with wheels can be moved around the garden according to season, or when needed as an impromptu guest room or a children's play zone. They can even be towed to another destination, for use as a mini holiday home.

From renovated vintage shepherd's huts and Romany caravans, to bespoke re-creations of traditional showman's carriages or workmanlike steam-engine caravans, many traditional mobile homes are being reinterpreted for contemporary living. Modern home comforts such as heating, lighting and basic cooking facilities are a welcome addition to otherwise untouched designs that have endured for centuries.

SHED STYLE

What goes on in the shed includes everything from conventional office work to highly creative artistic pursuits – and many things in between. A cabin away from the main house is the ideal place in which to store and use a treasured collection of childhood games; a sensible spot for indulging in messy hobbies such as model making or painting; and a great option for sleeping/guest space for visitors. Whether you are working, creating or relaxing, there are myriad shed styles to consider.

RIGHT Simply designed clapboard sheds make versatile home offices, guest cabins or entertaining spaces.

working

spaces

the home office

Tailor-made to meet your requirements, a working space may range in scale from a contemporary mini office or a light-filled design studio, to a makeshift but practical desk in a corner of the garden shed.

ABOVE RIGHT Colours can have a profound effect on your productivity. Blue, which is soothing and balancing, is a great colour to choose for a home-office shed.
OPPOSITE In small spaces, economical use of furniture and storage, plus a tidy approach, is necessary. A scaled-down desk will help.

Working from home has its obvious benefits, but it can be a tricky balancing act. Many home workers find the most challenging aspect of their day is to keep home and work life separate. Children, chores, domestic paperwork and the demands of daily living can be very distracting, so it is vital to create a place where you can mentally log on and concentrate.

What better place to be productive than in the peace and quiet of a shed at the bottom of the garden? There is no crushing commute. Just a few paces down the garden path, and you're there. It's no wonder that one in ten people now work full-time from home, many choosing to spend their working day tucked away in a shed. But what is that makes the perfect shed office, and where's the best place to start?

The first thing to consider when you are creating your shed office is to decide who will use it and when. Do you want the space to have a dual function – perhaps doubling up as a guest room – or would you prefer to keep work and home and social life totally separate. Are the children allowed to use the office for homework and study, or is the shed for your eyes only? If you are planning to share the space, how much of your office do you want to hide when you are finished for the day? Treat your home office as seriously as you would a traditional office – you'll need to create a space that allows you to be a productive and focused worker.

Consider whether you will have to hold meetings in your office, in which case you should plan an inviting route to the front door that bypasses your home and personal front door, unless you are willing to have visitors traipse through your domestic areas in order to get to the shed. Lighting the pathway to the shed is a good idea if you find yourself working in the evenings or if the shed doubles up as a guest space or is used for additional storage. Low-voltage spotlights sunk into the ground work well.

WHERE TO WORK?

Think about where you want the shed to go. This calls for a delicate balance. You need to feel separate from the house – both physically and mentally – to prevent you being distracted by the hustle and bustle of domestic life. For security reasons, however, it is important to keep an eye on the shed when it is not in use. Of all the shed spaces, home offices contain the most valuable equipment – the further away your shed is from your house, the more attractive it will be to burglars. As

with all sheds, you need to think about security. While it is a good idea to be able to look out on some greenery, make sure that you don't engulf your shed in trees and shrubs that could become a security risk. For a home office, this is especially important, so check that your household policy covers any computer equipment kept in the shed. The insurance company will need you to cost the value of the items in your shed office accurately and may require you to install specific locks or other security measures such as outside lights for added protection.

A shed office ideally needs to be self-contained. Consider installing a kitchenette in one corner of your office, as well as a toilet and hand-washing facilities. It might seem excessive, but endless trips back to the main house will seriously eat into your work time and make it almost impossible to have any fruitful periods of work. Unless your occupation necessitates you being locked away from modern distractions, you will also need to be contactable. A phone line and Internet facilities are absolute musts for a shed office, even if they're simply an extension

from your main home. These and other office essentials such as computers and faxes will all need power, so getting connected to an electrical supply should be a priority.

KEEPING WARM AND COOL

Temperature and productivity go hand in hand. There are no hard-and-fast rules, but occupational health experts recommend that people feel most comfortable between 13°C (56°F) and 30°C (86°F), depending on how sedentary or strenuous their work is. For office work, which involves long periods of being deskbound, the ideal is a constant background temperature of no less than 16°C (61°F) – any lower than that and you will feel uncomfortable if you sit still for any significant period of time. Your ability to concentrate also drops if you are too cold, so it's doubly important to get your shed well insulated and heated. Convection heaters and oil-filled radiators both provide pleasant background heat at the flick of a switch. Equally, it is important not to be too hot in the summer months. Portable air-conditioning units are a costly and energy-hungry option, though, so think about alternative ways to keep your shed cool. You can quickly reduce unnecessary heat by switching off electrical equipment when not in use and installing blinds or shutters to keep the sun out. Keep doors and windows open for natural ventilation. Other options include installing ceiling fans, painting your shed roof with reflective paint or fitting heat-reflective film to the windows. The latter two options significantly reduce the amount of outside ambient heat that finds its way inside.

LEFT An imaginative architect-designed eco shed is both an interesting building and an inspiring work space.
OPPOSITE A grass roof provides insulation and warmth for this sleek contemporary home office in an urban garden.

STORAGE AND SHELVING

Adequate storage is absolutely vital for a home office. Clutter is not only unsightly, but it can also seriously affect your work performance and productivity. A home office needs to be as organized and efficient as any commercial office, so it is important to have a place for everything and everything in its place. Above all, you need to keep it looking professional. Try not to let domestic clutter invade your space, and don't fall into the trap of using your shed office for storing other things. Here are some of the items a typical home office might need in terms of storage.

A filing system

Whether it's a filing cabinet or box files, create a filing system for day-to-day use. These files need to be picked over on a regular monthly basis, to update or discard paperwork, and the filing system should contain only documents from the past two years. Shred any financially sensitive material.

Document storage

Paperwork and correspondence older than two years needs to be boxed up, labelled and stored. Most commercial offices are now working towards a paperless system, which means less clutter, but be sure to have back-ups of all important documents. If your shed office is small, these boxed documents can be kept in dry storage in the main house (e.g. in the loft or a cupboard).

Office supplies cupboard

Pens, staples, paper, hole punches – office supplies and stationery need to be organized but easily accessible. A dedicated cupboard or set of drawers is ideal, especially one on castors which can be wheeled under the desk when not needed. Make sure that your office supplies are within reasonable reach and restocked on a regular basis. If you are really short of space, store some of your office supplies elsewhere, but only those items that you need infrequently.

Contacts book

Forget scraps of paper. Transfer all names and addresses to an address book or the computer, to keep your contact details in check and readily available.

Pinboard

A pinboard is useful for ongoing reminders and postcards, but don't let it become a resting place for paperwork. Review the contents of your pinboard on a regular basis.

Shelves

Think about installing some form of fitted shelving or cubbyholes. These are ideal for keeping folders and files out of the way, especially in a small shed. Reference material that doesn't need to be accessed regularly can be stored in neat boxes at a higher level than day-to-day documents. All folders and files kept at shelf height need to be clearly labelled for ease of use.

Storage for office equipment

Computers, keyboards, faxes, photocopiers, printers and other office items can be easily stored away when not in use. This is especially useful if the shed space doubles as a guest bedroom or you need to keep equipment locked away from young children. It also keeps expensive items from providing a tempting target for potential burglars. To save you from having to endlessly unplug and plug in appliances, consider specialist workstations designed for this very purpose. These are often designed to look like a cupboard or armoire, and their doors are simply closed to keep your computer and its peripherals hidden from view.

Tidy wiring

Long, untidy lengths of electric cable and overloaded sockets are a health and safety hazard for your shed office. Make sure that you have all the plugs, phone outlets and switches you need, at the correct height and location. For a really neat job, use decorative trucking or conduit to hide the cables.

OPPOSITE **Work with what you have. Even the smallest shed can become a hive of activity.**
TOP RIGHT **Slick storage solutions keep this desk clear of piles of paper and other mess.**
RIGHT **Home offices contain valuable equipment – make sure that your shed is fully insured and these items are covered.**
FAR RIGHT **Take a break. Try to include a seating area to gather your thoughts.**

work/live space

Most of us dream of escaping the office and working from home. But few of us have the space. One London firm of architects has proven that downshifting and saying goodbye to the daily commuter grind need not mean the end of your day job.

It is amazing what happens in some people's sheds. Just ask the architects at Ecospace. Their sophisticated garden studios are being used for everything from a doctor's waiting room to a professor's library. Clients include graphic artists, musicians, psychiatrists, yacht designers, television presenters, lawyers, photographers and producers – all looking for a place in which to practise their profession.

Ecospace's sheds may be pretty, but the reasoning behind them is eminently practical. Many of the company's clients owned or rented offices elsewhere, but found that a working shed was a much more cost-effective and eco-friendly solution. It also scrapped the need for a spirit-crushing daily commute. Other clients already worked from home, but needed a space detached from domestic distractions.

As with all sheds, the beauty of an Ecospace studio is that it eliminates some of the sticky issues associated with a typical

LEFT A light-filled mezzanine level increases space in this home office.
ABOVE No stress, no traffic and a commute to an uplifting workplace
that takes less than two minutes.

house extension — consultant's fees, unpredictable builders and spiralling costs. Planning permission is often a sticking point when you need to extend your home, especially if your house is historically significant. Invest instead in a shed, and there is a good chance you won't face a nightmare applying for consent.

The structure of an Ecospace studio is manufactured off-site, keeping disruption and build time on your actual property to a minimum. Instead, in just a matter of days, you have a home office complete with a super-efficient heating system, low-wattage nickel downlighters and an electrical supply.

For many, however, the Ecospace studio becomes much more than a place to work. Alongside the integral workstation and

storage systems, a shower room, mezzanine sleeping area, kitchenette, wood-burning stove and fitted furniture can all be chosen by clients — everything you could possibly need to turn your shed into a slice of home.

Once you have decided to invest in such a shed, the layout and decorative possibilities allow plenty of scope for tailor-making the space to fit your needs. This work/live space is every bit as smart and sophisticated as an urban bachelor pad. Neat and clever storage is part of the decorative scheme, while a wood-burning stove provides a sense of comfort and warmth for daytime and evening work or relaxation. Getting down to work becomes a pleasure, yet it is also easy to switch to rest.

<small>ABOVE</small> An architect's studio includes an integral workstation in a contemporary style and neat open storage systems.
<small>RIGHT</small> Western red cedar cladding, sleek aluminium trims and a 'living roof' are functional design elements.

eco garden office

The building industry rarely fares well when it comes to impact on the environment, so it is a breath of fresh air to hear that constructing a home office in your garden can be a sensible, economic option that will not cost the earth.

This architect's office in Kent, England, definitely gets the green light when it comes to eco credentials. It has a sustainable timber structure and cedar cladding, environmentally friendly electrics, high-performance insulation and energy-efficient double glazing. The fact that you are working from home instead of hopping into your car for a nerve-frazzling trip to the office also does wonders for your carbon footprint.

The living 'green roof' is not only ecologically sound, but also reduces the visual impact of the studio – perfect if you live in a conservation or heritage area, and need to keep the council happy. Green roofs also have high heat and sound insulation values, making them an excellent all-round eco option.

Inside, sustainably sourced birch plywood was used to clad the walls. Not only does this complement the timber nature of the building's exterior, but it also eliminates the need for a painted plaster finish. The floor is ultra low-maintenance and constructed from eco-friendly wear-resistant rubber, while the super-efficient heating system conserves as much energy as possible. Low-wattage lighting only adds to the planet-friendly equation.

Even the foundations get the eco thumbs-up, as a clever engineering system removes the need for a conventional concrete foundation. This shed stands on adjustable bearing shoes that not only minimize site disturbance, but dramatically reduce the need for environmentally wasteful concrete. What more could you ask?

creative

spaces

space to create

Sheds make fantastic creative spaces where we can be imaginative, original, inventive and purposeful, without any outside interference – places in which to pursue pleasures and pastimes such as music making, writing a novel or throwing pots.

OPPOSITE Fill your shed with favourite objects, plants, books and paintings, to fire your creative imagination.
ABOVE RIGHT Creative spaces call for clever storage, as a messy shed will affect your motivation and definitely slow your output.

Much of our daily life is about routine or responsibility, so it is a great treat to be able to design and create a space where we can really let go and be ourselves.

Garden sheds have long been a place of inspiration for artists, musicians and writers. From inventor Trevor Bayliss, tinkering away on his wind-up radios, to Benjamin Britten composing masterpieces, many of history's most talented people found inspiration and innovation at the bottom of their gardens. Dylan Thomas, Roald Dahl, Louis de Bernières, Rudyard Kipling, Philip Pullman, Agatha Christie, Arthur Miller and Charles Dickens all penned bestselling novels from their huts, while Harley and Davidson created their first motorcycle in a backyard shed. Sheds have even captured the imagination of a famous museum. London's Victoria and Albert Museum recently brought together a group of contemporary artists and designers to transform ten garden sheds into creative and conceptual spaces.

Unlike houses, sheds offer us the chance to build a creative room from scratch – one that can be as noisy, messy and chaotic as we please. All manner of joyful activities can take place in a shed – music, photography, art, woodwork, pottery, stained glass, flower arranging, collecting, model building … anything we like, really. We can glue, stick, draw, cut, scratch, scrape, mould, spray and sprinkle to our heart's content. And, when we are finished for the day, we can simply down tools and wander back up the garden path to civilization. Perfect.

But how do you go about making a creative space? Much will depend on the nature of your hobby or interest, but there are some general rules to follow if you want to make the most of your shed.

Consider the location, size and structure of your shed, where and how you will work inside, and suitable storage options, as well as lighting and creating the right atmosphere for your particular creative pursuit.

Above left **This oak tree house enjoys uninterrupted panoramic views and is the ideal setting for work and play.**
Above centre **Room with a view. Looking out onto the garden can be a great source of stimulation and an aid to thoughtful reflection.**

Above right **Writing, composing and other reflective pursuits often benefit from an isolated spot in the garden.**
Opposite **This summer house, perched on the edge of a lily pond, is a wonderful spot from which to watch wildlife.**

LOCATION

You need to make a space that supports your creativity. To do that, your shed should offer you lots of stimulation without too many distractions. A painter might want to make the most of any garden views, for example. Noisy hobbies such as metalwork need to be located away from neighbours, while pastimes that use lots of heavy or cumbersome materials should be located near a convenient access point for deliveries. If you are planning to store a lot of valuable items in your shed, this can dictate your choice of location – perhaps closer to the house, or away from any natural screening such as trees and shrubs within the garden. Additional outdoor security lighting is a good idea.

Quiet pursuits, such as writing. painting or composing, which require maximum concentration and minimum disturbance, will almost certainly need an isolated spot in the garden, away from the hustle and bustle of domestic life, and protected from intrusive noise. A shed on stilts may

be appropriate in a sloping garden or site. This option also works when a shed is to be used as a children's playroom, as it leaves space beneath the structure for playing games and outdoor toys.

SIZE AND STRUCTURE

Think about the size of the creative space you need. Does your hobby require a large floor area or tall ceilings? Does the shed floor need reinforcing? Certain activities, such as woodworking or sculpture, often need generous working space, while artists and photographers can pursue their interests with little more than a small seating area. Do you want the flexibility to be able to leave work 'in progress', or will you have to pack everything away and clean up every time?

Think, too, about how much natural light is necessary and how the nature of that light will be affected by the time of year and the climate in which you live. Depending on the quality and intensity of natural light

Natural light not only makes us feel good, but can enhance our working environment with a better sense of space.

you want, you can orient the position of your shed to gain the most benefit from the sun's path through the sky. You may need French windows, sliding glass doors or skylights, to maximize light – and to allow easy transport of bulky materials. Inside, natural light can be reflected throughout your creative space by using light paint colours, mirrors and light window treatments.

Creative spaces need to be constructed from materials that are suitable for the activity within. Soundproofing is a good idea for a home music studio, while fireproof considerations come into play if you plan on using a blowtorch for pursuits such as stained-glass making. See page 194 in Making Space for details on suitable options for sustainable and durable materials.

Messy activities may need a more robust shed than usual. Are you going to be able to clean up easily? Wipe-clean surfaces, durable materials and tough, sturdy furniture last much longer than traditional domestic tables and chairs under these conditions.

Even with careful forward planning, you may still discover that you need to modify your shed as time goes by – sometimes you can only discover what makes an effective creative space by spending time in it.

CREATIVE WORKING

Many crafts and hobbies need a workbench, where tools, supplies and equipment can be safely stored and used. As the bench will be a working surface, too, it is important to keep all your tools and equipment stored within reach on the wall at the back of the workbench or in handy drawers underneath. Clear labelling and a logical storage system will go a long way towards keeping it all in

order. Being organized actually helps most people be creative – if you have to spend too long scrabbling around for the right brush, pen or tool, motivation soon vanishes.

If you do not need a workbench, think about the kind of work surface you do need. Would a desk, drawing board, easel, sewing table or trestle table be more useful? What about working on the floor or utilizing the walls or ceiling? Can you simply work from a chair or a daybed, futon or beanbag?

STORAGE

Creative spaces benefit from good storage for materials and equipment. Think about the scale and type of materials you need to store. In a small space such as a shed, you need to make your storage count.

As well as the usual options such as shelves, cupboards and drawers, think about storing items in unusual places such as the ceiling void or the space above the door. Furniture such as benches, trunks and coffee tables that double up as storage are another useful option. And make use of reclaimed furniture such as freestanding glass-fronted display cabinets for fabric scraps, electrical equipment or fragile artwork. Don't be afraid to hang tools and equipment from the walls, or to use Shaker-style peg rails, which can hold bags, clothing, mirrors and even chairs. Simple hooks and racks also make great shed storage, especially for items you need to have close to hand. A shelf perched above them will provide additional storage. Cardboard boxes, plastic tubs, baskets and bags all add to your options, and can be part of a display wall as well as a storage solution. Have fun being inventive, and ideas will start to flow as you play with the space.

OPPOSITE Personalize your shed with colourful items to lift your spirits and help your creative spirit feel at home.
RIGHT If you work better without the distraction of 'things', keep the interior plain and simple.

INSPIRATION

Fill your shed with visual elements that inspire your creativity – photographs, drawings, pictures, plants, mirrors, favourite objects. An 'ideas pinboard' – where you display random inspirational images and thoughts – is a really useful spur for your imagination. Think about creating a 'thinking space'. This can take the form of a comfy chair and favourite throw or quilt; a window seat with a view, plus a basket of inspiring reference books; or a collection of special objects placed near your work desk to help the ideas to flow. Do you like to work to music? If so, remember to include a music system or radio in your plans.

The decoration can provide inspiration too. Colours can have a profound effect on mood and productivity levels, so pick one that makes you feel calm but alert. Colour psychologists suggest greens and blues are good choices for working in, as both of these are soothing and balancing. The particular shade of a colour also has a dramatic impact on its effect. So, experiment with how a colour makes you feel. If that all sounds like too much hard work, you cannot go wrong with off-whites and neutrals – both of which will add a wonderful feeling of natural light and a neutrality that provides a blank canvas on which to project your ideas.

Even fragrance can encourage creativity. Certain stimulating essential oils – such as basil, lemon, peppermint and rosemary, for example – are thought to be effective in increasing concentration, as well as being appealing scents for the space itself.

It is also important to keep 'idea traps' to hand – items such as a pad and pencil, or a voice-activated tape recorder, that allow you to record any moments of inspiration. Above all, a creative space needs to feel as if it is yours. Make that happen by personalizing it with things that matter to you.

LIGHTING

Natural light has a wonderful effect on people. Daylight and well-being go hand in hand. Sunlight has long been known to lift our spirits and energize us. Natural light increases our body's production of the neurotransmitter serotonin, which not only makes us feel cheerful, but also affects our ability to be creative. It's important, therefore, to encourage the flow of natural light into your creative shed space, unless you specifically need to work in a dark or dimly lit space. Activities such as painting and flower arranging, and close detailed work such as embroidery and sewing, benefit from being carried out in natural light, so place work desks close to windows and keep the windows unadorned if possible.

Artificial lighting for creative spaces works best as a combination of ambient and task lighting. For ambient lighting, uplighters are a better choice, and easier to install in a shed, than a central pendant light. Uplighters focus light upwards, towards the walls and ceilings, and won't create annoying shadows or reflections on your workspace. You will also need a focused task light to prevent eye strain – an adjustable desk lamp such as an Anglepoise or a clip-on spotlight is ideal. You can supplement the creative ambience with mood lighting such as fairy lights.

LEFT A space dedicated to a creative hobby allows you to leave work 'in progress'.
OPPOSITE Task lighting needs to be flexible and adaptable – an Anglepoise lamp is ideal.

CREATIVE CONDITIONS

Think about the conditions that help you to be creative. Where do you work best? Do you need a dark space or plenty of natural light? Do you like to hear outside noises or do you need absolute silence? Does the temperature affect your creativity? Many people find that they cannot feel creative if they do not feel comfortable. Does time of day influence your hobby? If so, can you build a shed that makes the most of the morning, afternoon or evening? Would you like to be able to work there at night, if the mood strikes you? Does what you see out of the window affect your mood? Do you want to feel connected to nature, or would you prefer to hear people and traffic noise?

Do you want to see the house from your shed, or would you prefer to feel hidden from view? Many people overlook the concept of 'reverse views' – in other words, what you see from the bottom of your garden when you look back towards the house. This is a vital part of the overall scheme and something you need to consider when looking at where to site the shed and how it relates to the main house.

Comfortable seating is crucially important, particularly if you are to spend long hours in your shed. From ergonomic chairs for working, to sofas for reclining – choose wisely. Favourite cushions can be brought

from the main house to your creative den, as can favourite cups and mugs. Bringing the outside in with special vases of flowers picked from the garden, potted plants and the colours of nature makes you feel more connected to the landscape and therefore more relaxed and ready to create.

Think about what you see outside from the windows of your shed – try to ensure the best views possible, making the most of the positioning of any trees, plantings and other garden features. You'll also need to take into account any shade that the shed creates, and adjust the planting accordingly. Laurels, bamboo, ivy, box, dogwood, hellebores, hostas, ferns and mahonias all like shady or part-shady conditions. But a quick chat with someone at your local garden centre will soon reveal the range of trees, shrubs and plants that will do very well in shade in your area. Plant them up in containers, so that you can vary your view according to the seasons.

Sheds are ideal candidates for trellises and pergolas. These allow you to train any number of climbers and vines around the building, for privacy, comfort and inspiration in equal measure. For a pergola, consider a vine or climber that provides shade during the warmer months, but dies back during winter, to let through sunlight unimpeded.

Indoors again, contemplate having some means of listening to music, whether its an old-fashioned gramophone, a sleek iPod or a portable radio that can live in the shed.

Opposite above left Fabric on walls and under a worktop provides inspiration for a wild imagination in this tiny space.
Opposite below left Floor- to-ceiling glass lets in ample light for floral creativity.
Opposite below right A veritable cottage-garden den provides a sense of escape in a shed crammed with inspiring items.
Right A coat of white paint gives this craft shed a feeling of space and light, ideal when working with fabrics and colour.

ABOVE Gathering ideas for the creation of a homewares collection.
RIGHT The garden is a constant and ever-changing source of design inspiration.
OPPOSITE Linda's light-filled studio brings the spirit of Atlantic Seaboard architecture to the London suburbs.

designer's studio

Interior designers spend their lives creating gorgeous spaces for other people to enjoy. But what do they choose for their own homes? A shed at the bottom of Linda Barker's garden reveals her passion for light and space, and a love of the outdoors.

Living amid the hectic pace and noisy flurry of a major city such as London, it can be difficult to find the emotional and physical space to be creative. For British interior designer and television presenter Linda Barker, a shed has turned out to be the perfect solution to the need for an inspirational thinking space.

Nestling in a secluded part of her London garden, behind a fig tree, this little wooden shed provides Linda with the perfect balance of solitude and inspiration. Tucked around a corner, out of sight of the main house, the shed sits comfortably among the herb and vegetable beds. Here, Linda can shut out the distractions of home life and get down to the nuts and bolts of her design work, whether it is developing a new line for her award-winning Really Linda Barker home accessories range or creating an interior for one of her many clients.

Designed and built by Homelodge, an award-winning family-run business that Linda found at the London Ideal Home Show,

the shed is both practical and pretty. According to the company, these attractive timber lodges are regularly pressed into service as offices, studios, granny annexes, guest rooms, playrooms and even affordable starter homes.

Linda's own lodge has a strong East Coast feel – clad in weatherboard and painted in one of Linda's favourite shades, duck egg blue. Linda often uses what she calls a 'spring palette' both inside and out. Not only do her favourite blues, creams and naturals soften the austerity of an otherwise pared-down space, but she also finds them calming and restful.

When it comes to the practicalities, building the shed could not have been easier. It was largely constructed off-site, then quickly assembled in a couple of days. The only preparation work required in the space itself was the footings for the foundations. This kept disruption to a minimum and meant that her much-loved garden, with its abundance of greenery, was

largely unaffected by the new addition. It also meant that her design studio could be up and running in a fraction of the time it would take to build a regular house extension.

The fact that Linda's studio was created swiftly in no way means that it isn't as warm and comfortable as any permanent dwelling. With excellent double glazing and insulation, the shed easily meets current building regulations. The timbers have also been pressure-impregnated with preservative to provide protection against the worst that the British weather can throw at it and to improve its longevity.

As Linda is an interior designer, a key factor in her decision-making process was the style of the shed. Living in a city filled with stone and brick architecture, she particularly relished the idea of working in a rustic timber-framed building filled with lots of light. Keen to keep the interior as bright and breezy as the exterior, Linda used pale cream walls to reflect light, a large

ABOVE Keep to keep things light and bright,
Linda opts for pale colours and a large glass-
topped table.
OPPOSITE Rattan furniture, terra-cotta pots,
potted plants and objets trouvés bring in a
sense of the outdoors.

glass table, and rattan chairs for an airy atmosphere inside. A sea-grass carpet and a few well-chosen accessories finish the effortlessly chic informal look.

When it came to planning how to use the space, Linda chose deliberately not to overcomplicate the interior specifications of the shed with built-in furniture or complicated wiring. Rather than install tons of technology, she wanted to keep the shed simple and contemplative, so that it could be used primarily as a drawing space. And, while it is easy enough to whisk her laptop or phone down the garden and into the shed, that is not the point – the shed performs the important function of being an escape from all the usual distractions that technology brings.

Linda was born and brought up in rural Yorkshire, in England's north. It comes as no surprise, then, that the shed's connection to the garden is an integral and important one, especially on warm summer days when Linda likes to work with the shed doors flung wide open, to let in both light and heat.

On these warmer days, the outdoor space becomes an extension of the shed and an endless source of inspiration. And, at the end of a busy working day, the shed also has an alter ego, doubling as the ideal spot to host a barbecue party on balmy evenings.

But Linda is not the only one who gets to enjoy this secret hideaway. Knowing that teenagers like their privacy, Linda lets her daughter use the shed for sleepovers and movie nights. Happy in the knowledge that she is only a few steps away up the garden path, Linda can give her daughter and friends the freedom they crave, without creating havoc for the rest of the household.

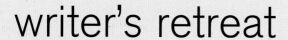

ABOVE **Small drawers house stationery and ensure a tidy desk.**
RIGHT **A reclaimed beach hut complete with serving hatch offers simple comfort and a home for new ideas.**
OPPOSITE **With its battered leather seating and ticking cushions, this 'thinking space' is comfortable enough for taking afternoon tea or even a nap when inspiration is lacking.**

writer's retreat

Writing tends to be a solitary pursuit, one that pretty much requires complete absorption. A quiet haven at the bottom of the garden is the ideal place to pen a masterpiece or simply scribble some inspiring thoughts.

Here, a shabby beach hut has been pressed into service, as calm as the sea and as cosy as a fisherman's sweater. Sitting on shingle and raised up on railway sleepers, this dry-docked shed offers more than enough peace to engender a productive environment, without the need to travel far from home.

A distinctly retro feel permeates the space. A well-worn leather sofa and armchair provide snug seating, and are teamed with contrasting striped ticking cushions and velvet seat covers. An old blanket chest placed on a white rug on top of the bare floorboards serves as an excellent coffee table-cum-storage box. A reclaimed vegetable crate, complete with a coat of white paint, has become a utilitarian storage solution for magazines, while simple wall-mounted shelves keep the author's pens and pencils in an orderly fashion. Multiple task lighting allows the owner to read and write well into the night should the mood hit, with the option of a quick restorative nap.

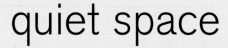

ABOVE **Malcolm keeps his shed defiantly free of computers and other forms of distracting modern technology.**
OPPOSITE **The shed is named 'Lavender Halt', after Malcolm's prized Hornby O-gauge model railway set, which runs along one of the shed's shelves.**

quiet space

For one British artist, replacing a worn-out shed on a small budget and within a conservation area was to become an object lesson in reducing, reusing and recycling.

According to artist Malcolm Temple, every man has at least one shed in him. At the far end of his garden squatted the usual brown shed, rotting from the ground up and the roof down, and crammed with spiders and junk. In defiance of the thoughtless waste today's consumer society encourages, Malcolm decided that recycling materials was a priority and vowed that the shed would cost no more than a few hundred pounds to design and build, including planning fees.

Scouring building sites and skips, plus the vigilance of friends, led to amazing discoveries – rolls of insulation, brand-new flooring, patio doors and even cut-glass windows from a pub refurbishment. Six months of scavenging, hauling and lifting later, he had his stash. Three months more of solitary labour, and the shed was complete and watertight. With no technology here to distract, Malcolm sits in stillness: thinking, dreaming and sketching. His mantra: 'Travel slowly. Enjoy the view.'

garden

spaces

a place to potter

A garden shed is the perfect hideaway for any keen gardener. Whether it is used for storing tools or potting up plants, this is an unmistakably natural space for anybody with green fingers – a place to sow seeds, nurture cuttings and pore over gardening books.

ABOVE RIGHT A terra cotta tiled floor makes a handsome but hard-wearing choice for a well-used potting shed.
OPPOSITE If you do not have space for a shed, a garden tidy will keep all your tools and seed trays safely stored.

Creating a garden shed needs to balance practicality with pleasure. After all, gardening is as much about relaxation as it is about roses. So what do you need to think about when creating a perfect garden room?

When siting the shed, take into account the position of the sun at different times of the day. If you are intending to work with plants, you'll need to consider the amount of sunlight that hits the garden room, and its strength. You'll also need to consider factors that create unwanted shade, especially during spring and autumn, when the sun is low in the sky. Look out for nearby trees and hedges, the position of any other garden buildings and the location of the house.

Conversely, you also need to think about providing shade when the sun is too strong. Too much sunlight will make your garden room unbearably hot, and scorch any plants that you are cultivating, particularly if you live in a hot, sunny climate. Many solar sheds come with shading kits for this purpose, but

roller blinds or canvas shades work well too. If you are going to heat the garden shed, it will need to be near a supply of electricity or mains gas, or are you planning to have self-contained heating? Electricity may be necessary for other reasons such as lighting, so it might be worth pricing the option of getting connected to the house supply.

What about access to water? This is especially important if you have a vegetable patch nearby. If the shed is any distance from the house, you won't want to rely on a hosepipe running the length of the garden. Consider getting a permanent supply fitted nearer the shed, as an outside tap, or even having water and drainage installed in the shed itself. If this option is too expensive, a water butt is a cost-effective, eco-friendly alternative. Connect one or more butts to the gutters on the roof of your shed, and you can store as much rainwater as you need. If young children use your garden, always choose a water butt that has a childproof lid.

the interior and the exterior, taking as much care over the decoration and paint scheme as you would for a room in your house. Other considerations should be not only where you are going to put your tools of the trade, but also how often you use them. Some gardening items need to be ready-to-hand all year round; others can be safely stored for only seasonal use. Remember the gardening basics – lawn mower, hosepipe, wheelbarrow, watering cans, plant pots, compost, seed trays, hand tools such as clippers and trowels, gardening gloves and gardening twine, among other things.

Making a garden shed both comfortable and functional is a creative process in which you can experiment with storage and layout, keeping all your tools and equipment close to hand, while creating a compact gardening space for seed germination, potting and taking cuttings. If you are going to use the shed for cultivating and growing plants, you may also need to think about installing some form of heating to maintain them.

Opposite **Whether you want to store your tools, sow seeds, take cuttings or slip in a well-earned nap, this stylish, compact shed is contemporary but comfortable.**
Above **Simple lightweight curtains provide much-needed shade for this garden shed.**
Right **Antique-style galvanized washtubs in varying sizes make for stylishly quirky but robust planters.**

Traditionally, garden sheds have often been repositories for rusty lawn mowers and unwanted plant pots, places where no one ventured very often and where discarded items of furniture and outdoor paraphernalia languished. Often they have become so cramped that the space no longer functions as anything more than an outdoor cupboard. Nowadays, if you want to get the most from your garden shed, you will need to plan both

doesn't tend to lend itself to seating here. That doesn't mean you cannot introduce fabrics to the space in the form of seat covers or throws. Just make sure they are removable, washable and fadeproof.

With some practical skill and a little bit of imagination, you can also make 'new' pieces of furniture using reclaimed wood offcuts from discarded pieces of furniture.

RECYCLED FURNITURE

The garden shed is the perfect place to recycle, reuse and reinvent discarded items of storage, reclaimed or salvaged furniture, painted bric-a-brac, and seating. The battered charm of rediscovered tables, chairs, vegetable crates and careworn baskets creates a comfortable and effortless style at the bottom of the garden, where gardening is best enjoyed at a leisurely pace.

A comfortable seating area is a wonderful addition to a garden shed, and the ideal spot to browse through reference books or seed catalogues. If space is at a premium, a dual-purpose garden bench is very useful. Whether it's a bench with wicker storage baskets underneath or a lift-up seat and deep storage compartment, there are numerous designs from which to choose, all of which can be softened with a padded seat or scatter cushions.

Another practical option is a foldaway garden chair, which can be stored on a peg rail when not in use, or a brightly coloured deck chair. As the garden shed is such as functional space, upholstered furniture

STORAGE AND DISPLAY

Gardening is a dirty job, so it is best not to waste money on expensive storage boxes. Reclaimed wooden crates, jute sacks, apple racks, trugs, baskets, enamel tins, rubber buckets and heavy-duty plastic containers all make tough, practical and attractive storage options. Specialist garden storage also comes in many forms, including seed packet organizers and twine stands. Enjoy a browse through local garden centres, and pick out storage options that work best for you.

If you find that you have a large amount of garden items that need storing, or that the family wants somewhere to keep extra items such as bicycles, garden furniture and barbecues, consider getting a 'garden tidy' in addition to a garden shed. Working effectively in a shed that is overstuffed is impossible; a garden tidy (in essence, a large outdoor cupboard without windows) provides a generous amount of storage and keeps your gardening room a workable, enjoyable space. Your local hardware shop or DIY store is the probably the quickest and cheapest place to source a garden tidy, although bespoke versions are available through specialist companies.

Your shed's floor area should remain as clear as possible. Lots of garden items lend themselves to being stored on Shaker-style peg rails or shelves. Everything from spades to garden seating can be stored on the walls of your shed, leaving room for manoeuvring at floor level. Gardening tools and equipment can be heavy, so you'll need to make sure that the fixings and shed walls are strong enough to take the extra weight.

Some garden items need careful storage, especially if you have small children. Most garden sprays, weed killers and fertilizers are poisonous and need to be stored away from little hands. Keep all chemicals under lock and key, even ones made up of natural

ABOVE **Keep your shed floor as clear as possible with plenty of wall-mounted pegs, shelving and storage cupboards.**
OPPOSITE **Save your money for seeds. Apple racks, cardboard boxes and jute bags all provide cheap and cheerful storage options.**

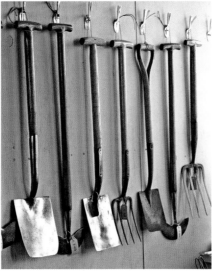

ingredients. Organic sprays can often be just as potent as chemical versions – that is why they are so effective in the garden. You will also need to lock away all sharp tools such as topiary shears, garden forks, secateurs and electric or petrol strimmers.

Once you have sorted through all your belongings, you can decide which items can be readily stored on the wall and which are better on shelving, which could form part of a display themselves, and those that really need to be hidden or locked away for safety or aesthetic reasons.

TOOLS OF THE TRADE

Garden tools can be surprisingly aesthetic when suspended on vintage coat hooks in regimented rows against shed walls or on Shaker-style peg rails, in a functional yet beautiful manner. Create a custom-made storage system by setting upturned pots in varying sizes between chunky wooden planks, to double up as shelves and supports (see left). You can see what you need at a glance, as well as enjoying the pleasing display. Some modern-day tools are valuable, especially large electrical items

Above Leaves love light – if you want to grow plants in your garden shed, you need a generous expanse of glass to let in natural light.
Above right Reclaim and reuse – this old washstand has been pressed into service as a workbench.
Below right Too much sunlight will scorch your plants – think about providing vulnerable plants with shade and protection.
Opposite Zinc and enamel buckets are an attractive but eminently practical choice for gardeners.

such as lawn mowers, strimmers and pressure washers, so it is worth considering security for these items. Home insurance claims tend to rocket during the summer months, mostly as a result of an increase in garden thefts. You can easily deter thieves by locking away garden tools at the end of every day, and keeping your garden shed within sight of the house. Police often advise garden-shed owners to security-mark valuable items and install security lights on both the house and the shed. Check also whether your home insurance policy covers your shed contents, including expensive pieces of individual equipment.

GROWING AND PLANTING

A garden shed is essentially a working space, so you'll need to create a practical workbench or counter for sowing and potting up. A potting bench is usually constructed from timber, with gaps between the

planks to allow excess soil and water to fall through. It also has to be fairly sturdy, to cope with the weight of watered potted plants. The timber needs to be treated with preservative to cope with UV light and the long-term effects of moisture. Below-counter shelving is also a useful storage addition, as is a rack for storing small garden tools.

In the past, greenhouses were designed for growing tender plants while garden sheds (or potting sheds, as they are sometimes known) were primarily for tool storage and potting up. It soon becomes apparent, however, that a building in which both these activities could take place would be incredibly useful. Known as 'garden rooms' or 'solar sheds', these useful small structures have the best of both worlds – plenty of windows to let in light and warmth to encourage plant growth, combined with a dedicated workspace and generous interior wall space for storage. An added bonus of garden rooms is that, as they aren't entirely glazed, they tend to be more comfortable places in which to sit and relax.

LIGHTING NEEDS

Most flat-pack garden sheds come with either no window at all or only a small one as standard. On small sheds, it is not possible to open these windows, so bear this in mind when you are planning to purchase an off-the-shelf shed.

If you plan to use your shed to cultivate plants, it will need to let in significantly more natural light than usual if your plants are going to thrive. Look for a garden room that has a generous ratio of glazing to timber; it doesn't matter whether it's glazed roof panels, French windows, or wall-to-ceiling glazing. Just make sure that at least some of the windows can be opened, to improve ventilation (poor air circulation increases humidity and encourages plant disease).

HEATING THE SPACE

Depending on what you plan to grow or keep in your shed or garden room, and the climate in which you live, you'll need to look at your options for heating. Some plants will overwinter happily in an unheated building, while others require a consistent year-round temperature. The Royal Horticultural Society recommends electric heaters as the most adaptable source of heating for smaller garden rooms or greenhouses – and the most efficient means of maintaining specified temperatures. Unlike gas or kerosene heaters, these produce no fumes, so there is no need for ventilation when they are in use.

PLANTING UP

Seed trays, whether plastic or reclaimed, are vital for overwintering tubers and bulbs, and for bringing on seedlings and cuttings. Set up an area where you can leave trays undisturbed while you are cultivating plants, maybe at eye level and out of the way. It is really useful to have some space in which to experiment, and generally potter about. Try recycling flowerpots, and create an efficient storage system for different types of pots, labels, twine, and garden tools.

RUNNING WATER

In an ideal world, every potting shed would have a sink and running water, but this simply is not practical in most gardens. If this applies in your case, a water butt attached to the outside guttering will at least give you access to water for dampening compost around seedlings and for watering small plants. Keep a watering can, particularly one with a rose on the spout, handy.

ABOVE LEFT Be bold with your shed colour. Rich Scandinavian red makes a striking contrast against a garden's vivid greenery.
ABOVE RIGHT Chinese cobalt blue always makes a strong colour statement for any static elements of a garden.

OPPOSITE Nostalgic floral-printed fabrics and a duck-egg blue shed complement the colourful cottage-garden planting in this rural garden. The loose, almost wildflower-like planting is not overwhelmed by the sturdy structure of the shed, keeping the garden as the main focus.

COLOUR

Painting a shed is a good way to create a colourful feature in the garden, providing either a subtle backdrop or a statement piece to accompany the planting. Traditional heritage colours such as moss, lichen and cream chime well with predominantly green shrubs in a variety of shades and textures. They are particularly effective when herbs such as sage, lavender and chives are planted up next to them.

Vibrant colours are the answer when you want to create a visual statement, picking out the shed as a strong focal point in the garden. Strong blues and reds look best against a colourful planting scheme containing flowers such as the cottage-garden favourites of hollyhocks, delphiniums, lupins and foxgloves, or dahlias and the acid green tones of *Euphorbia* and *Alchemilla mollis*. These strong colours work equally well with rich Mexican or Mediterranean-inspired settings and plants such as bougainvillea, mimosa and hydrangeas, or the Caribbean-inspired shades found in cornflowers, delphiniums and red poppies.

There are a number of ways to treat or stain bare wood using colour. Certain timber, such as oak, can be left untreated if you prefer, or your shed may already come pre-finished. If you are painting it yourself, you can choose from any number of options, from subtle wood stains to bright gloss paints. Much will depend on the type and surface texture of the timber, but if you can opt for an eco-friendly option so much the better. Wood finishes, including paints, stains and varnishes, often contain high levels of volatile organic compounds (VOCs), which are known to cause air pollution and have been linked to health problems such as allergies and breathing difficulties. When you are choosing a wood finish, opt for one with the best eco credentials possible. Look for 'natural' paints or finishes with low or no VOC content. These paints often come in more muted shades. Where possible, avoid the use of timber preservative, as it can be extremely harmful to the atmosphere. When you have no option but to use it, shop around your local hardware store until you find the most eco-friendly type available.

SHEDS FOR ANIMALS

From shaggy dogs to posh poultry, sheds make ideal houses for animals. Both livestock and pets naturally thrive in timber buildings. Wooden structures breathe, providing just the right amount of shelter without the problems of condensation or overheating. Dogs, hens, ducks, pigeons, rabbits, horses, cows – all manner of domestic animals flourish in these structures. A prettily painted chicken coop or dog kennel can be a charming addition to a garden, but animal welfare and good husbandry should always take precedence over the picturesque. One design can never fit all. Animals are also very choosy, so it's important to take great care to provide just the right creature comforts.

Hens Chicken coops or henhouses are probably the most popular sheds for animals. Good-quality housing is absolutely vital if you want to keep poultry healthy and happy. A shed for hens needs to be sturdy enough to cope with bad weather and secure enough to deter foxes, badgers and other predators. It's amazing what a determined predator will chew through to get to your flock, so opt for heavy-gauge mesh wire instead of the usual chicken wire. All the timber in your chicken shed needs to be treated to lengthen its life, but make sure that any wood preservatives are safe for your hens. Tanalith E, a chrome- and arsenic-free timber preservative, has been shown to be safe for both animals and the environment. If you decide to paint your henhouse, again make sure that any wood finishes are safe to use with animals. All metal fixings, such as bolts and hinges, will need to be galvanized to prevent rust.

The ideal henhouse should also be slightly raised off the ground on pilings, to prevent cold and damp penetrating upwards through the floor. If you have the option, site your henhouse near trees to offer your flock shade in the hot months and protection from

OPPOSITE Posh poultry – these hens have an entire 'street' of sheds to themselves.
LEFT Ducks require similar housing conditions to those of chickens.
BELOW Henhouses and coops require an 'elevated' position, to keep out cold and damp, and encourage ventilation.

wind and rain. Sizewise, you need to allow at least one square foot per hen, plus an area for nesting and a perch.

Cleanliness is also essential with poultry. Construct the shed with an access door large enough to allow you to clean without too much bother. Hobby henkeepers often recommend lining the floor of your hen house with newspaper, followed by a thin layer of wood shavings or straw.

the potting shed

All gardeners are at their happiest in the potting shed. A place of quiet industry where the true alchemy of cultivation takes place, the potting shed is the hub of any garden.

From the starting point of an unpromising packet of seeds, gardeners sow, water and watch minor miracles happen under their very noses. Potting sheds are the place where seedlings get their start in life before being moved on to the next stage, whether it is a temporary residence in an adjacent greenhouse or outside into the big wide world.

A true potting shed needs certain elements to allow this magic to take place. Forget expensive containers and designer fabrics, a potting shed needs to be practical above all else. Whether it's filling seed trays with compost or transplanting seedling plugs to pots, there is likely to be soil flying in all directions, so you will need surfaces and accessories that can take a beating and be easily cleaned or swept.

A brick, stone or terra cotta tiled floor is the perfect starting point – any stray compost can simply be swept out of the door and into the garden. Muddy plant pots are a regular feature of

potting sheds and, while they should really be kept outside and washed before being brought inside, a hard floor will take endless washing if things get really messy. As most potting sheds are not heated or protected against moisture, a stone or brick floor is one of the only types of flooring robust enough to stand semi-outdoor conditions.

Storage is an absolute priority too. You will need to dedicate at least one wall to racks or shelving. On these you can stack all your seed trays, string, watering cans, pens and pencils, labels and pots, keeping the floor space as clear as possible. The small items you regularly use – such as twine, gloves and scissors – should be hung from a rail or kept in place by tracing an outline on the wall under each hook. If possible, keep any large garden tools out of the way in a different shed.

If you are planning to store seeds, there are a number of factors worth bearing in mind. If you are saving seeds from your garden, once they are clean they need to be packed into dry envelopes, or cloth bags for large seeds, and labelled with the name of the plant and the date. Seeds can also be stored in an airtight containers, such as a jam jar with a screw-top lid. In both cases, seeds need storing in a cool, dry place. A small mini-fridge is ideal if you have a power supply to your potting shed – otherwise a very dry, dark corner will do. Just be sure to keep checking the packets to make sure that your stored seeds are not rotting or being damaged in any way.

Experienced gardeners usually like to have somewhere to keep their dry compost to hand and a separate space for potting up. Take expert gardener Monty Don's potting shed, for example. He has one bench against a wall with a dry supply of loam, compost and coir spread in different bays (large bins labelled and tucked underneath the potting bench would work equally well). Opposite that, Monty also has another bench with

inbuilt wooden trays filled with different potting mixes. The best potting benches are positioned at a comfortable standing height and deep enough to take a number of seed trays at once. It is important to leave a generous gap between any benches, however, as you may need access in and out of your potting shed with a wheelbarrow. In terms of construction, most potting benches are made from robust, treated timber, but a stone slab or stainless-steel surface is equally good and very easy to care for.

Potting sheds create mess, so ideally you could incorporate washing facilities for rinsing hands and tools. An old Belfast or butler's sink is ideal, but don't worry if it has the odd chip or blemish – the potting shed is about plants, not perfection. Access to a cold-water supply is also essential for watering any cuttings or seedlings. Lighting is something to consider. Seeds can be tiny and difficult to see in fading light. A sunny window will provide most of the rays you need, but it is always useful to have an additional source of lighting for rainy days or those twilight potting sessions. An overhead light can cast unwanted shadows over your potting bench, so consider task lighting such as an Anglepoise lamp instead.

Beyond that, how you decorate your potting shed is up to you. Some people go all out to create the perfect garden haven – soft armchair and kettle included. For others, a simple radio is all the embellishment they need.

LEFT A robust stone sink is a natural companion for a busy potting bench.
OPPOSITE A hard floor surface is a must for any gardening room – spilt soil or compost can be quickly swept up and out of the door.

relaxing

spaces

getting away from it all

The best sheds for relaxation are those that do not contain the trappings of working life. Step back from the rat race, leave the computer, TV, phone and mobile for other spaces, and focus on creating a place for simple pleasures.

ABOVE Catch a rare moment of seclusion in a relaxing shed by the river, faithful canine companion by your side.
OPPOSITE Weatherboard walls, pared-down accessories and rustic furnishings create a soothing homelike atmosphere.

Why is it so difficult these days to relax? We all need space to unwind, but our houses are perhaps not the easiest places to find peace and quiet. Many of us feel ill at ease with our living spaces: endless chores greet us on our return from work; piles of paperwork demand attention; even being part of a family can be as wearing as it is wonderful, with other people's needs taking precedence over your own.

For many, the solution is to find relaxation away from domestic chaos, spending a soothing hour at a day spa or pounding away on a treadmill. But what if you could have all the blissful isolation you need without all the expense and hassle of a trip to the gym? More and more people are transforming their sheds into relaxation spaces. From meditation rooms to reading huts, yoga and pilates studios to saunas and massage rooms, Sheds are fast becoming an important antidote and a smart solution to the stresses and strains of everyday life.

It makes perfect sense. As we saw in the introduction to this book, one of a shed's most appealing attributes is its separateness from the main house. Escaping involves nothing more than a few steps across the lawn, but it might as well be the other side of the world. Our shed becomes a place where we can enjoy moments of rare solitude, whether it's reading a book uninterrupted or mediating in silence. Only by having a place to be ourselves at rest can we take time to renew our energies and refresh feelings of balance and focus.

To create a relaxing shed, think about its use before planning how to furnish and decorate it. A waterside fishing hut or beach house will need durable furniture and furnishings that will bear some exposure to the elements, while a meditation space or yoga room calls for pared-down decoration and perhaps a pale colour scheme for the walls and floor, to aid the mind-clearing exercise for which the space is intended.

RELAXING COLOURS

Colour has a profound effect on our ability to relax. It works on our moods in two ways. The first is through 'association' – we connect colours with experiences and even particular feelings. Perhaps a certain colour makes us feel anxious because it reminds us of a spell in hospital or an unhappy time at school. A colour can also have a positive association, reviving good memories or reminding us of a favourite place. We also connect colour with things we experience in nature – the sky, sea and plants, for example.

CREATING CALM

Choosing colour carefully for your relaxing shed is important. Colour can affect us on a physiological level. Numerous tests have found that colours can have a profound effect on the brain; we already know, for example, that certain colours have the power to suppress appetite, calm violent behaviour, and even affect how we taste food. When it comes to painting the interior of your shed, you'll need to think about colours that will enhance any feelings of relaxation. Colours have subtly different effects on different people, but traditionally the most serene colours are generally the cool shades such as green and blue. Neutrals and earthy tones are also often used for relaxation spaces.

Remember to keep the furniture simple. It can be a relaxing process in itself to set about making your own simple shed furniture from discarded fruit and vegetable

LEFT A quiet spot in a summer house is a great solution for those times when you need to de-stress. OPPOSITE Handmade cushions on a decadent daybed make a perfect retreat from 21st-century living.

crates, storage pallets or reclaimed items. Paint the walls and floors a uniform colour to create a harmonious feeling of space and airiness, and use plain or striped fabrics for an unfussy feel.

CREATING COMFORT

Choosing fabrics that inspire you, or are easy to live with, will add to the sense of comfort and calm in your shed. For a delicate touch, combine plain fabrics with florals, soft sheers with linens, and coarse-woven rugs in natural fibres with pale painted wooden floors. Light muslin window coverings look good as a backdrop to robust but pleasing cotton or linen cushions on chairs or daybeds. Such simple fabrics sit well against ironwork, rattan or wooden furniture for easy comfort.

GETTING THE LIGHT RIGHT

Natural light and well-being go hand in hand. Sunlight influences many of our bodies' natural processes – sleep, libido, moods. We feel better and more relaxed when our body clock is in harmony with the innate patterns of day and night: in the morning, we feel energized by the sunrise; in the evening, we feel calmed and soothed by a slow sunset.

Psychologists and doctors have long understood the health benefits of light, and yet still most of us spend 90 per cent of our daily life stuck indoors, immersed in artificial light. It is little wonder that conditions such as seasonal affective disorder (SAD) are commonplace. Encourage natural light into your relaxation shed. Making the most of any available light will not only greatly enhance your enjoyment of the space, but also aid in the relaxation process. Position your shed to receive as much natural light as possible or to make the most of a particular time of day. As the sun travels from east to west, it makes good sense to orient your shed's windows according to the particular use you plan for the shed. If you want an early morning meditation space, east-facing windows or French windows will allow you to enjoy the sunrise. Equally, if you plan to relax in the early evenings, west-facing windows are preferable. If you want to use the space all day, south-facing windows will capture the majority of the day's rays if you live in the northern hemisphere, while the reverse is true for the southern hemisphere. Skylights and windows installed at an angle will also add an extra dimension, letting in light on even the dullest days.

FEELING THE HEAT

For most of us, relaxation is a sedentary or slow-moving exercise. It is important to get the ambient temperature in your shed right, or it will interfere with your ability to wind down. Our bodies feel most at ease

between 18°C (64°F) and 25°C (77°F) – any lower than that, and your body will have to work hard to keep warm, making it difficult to feel calm. Insulation is the key to keeping your relaxation shed cosy and ensuring that you are not wasting heat or money. Electric underfloor heating may also be a good option, as it can be installed on the top of solid timber floors, then either tiled or boarded over with floorboards, heat-resistant carpet or laminate flooring. This will make any floor-level exercise or stretches much more comfortable. A wood-burning stove is

another good option for a relaxation room. Nothing compares to the 'crackle factor' of a real log fire – just staring into the flames can become a kind of meditation in itself.

ZEN SPACES

Making a space where you can just sit back and be, in surroundings that readily induce calm and contemplation, is the aim of most people who create a relaxing haven in their garden. A space that is inviting yet at the same time provides views to the outer world is a great treat. Making the most of natural

ABOVE The principles of Zen design can help to create an oasis of calm in which to relax and recuperate.
OPPOSITE TOP LEFT Generously proportioned windows make the most of breathtaking views in this lakeside retreat.
OPPOSITE TOP RIGHT Top-hinged shutters double as windows, protecting this tropical shed from the unrelenting midday sun.
OPPOSITE BOTTOM RIGHT Natural fabrics complement bare wood panelling and doors in this pared-down hideaway.

light, using cushions to create comfortable seating areas and adding in plants to bring nature indoors are all simple but effective tools to use. Everyone differs, but most people find certain sounds comforting, such as trickling water, crashing waves, birdsong, wind chimes or rhythmic drumming. Instrumental music, such as certain forms of classical or jazz music, have also been shown to significantly reduce stress levels, so why not experiment with finding sounds that create a soothing shed?

Following some basic feng shui principles can often bring an unobtrusive sense of peace to a space. For garden design, there are differing recommendations for materials, planting and lines of vision, depending on the orientation of your building. It involves creating a balance of the flow of energy (chi), so that all the elements produce a positive, harmonious energy and do not dominate one over the other.

RELAXING SCENTS

Scent can play a vital role in creating a relaxing space. Smells can have a powerful therapeutic effect, making us feel calm, tranquil and peaceful. Fresh flowers, naturally scented candles, citrus peel, herbs and spices, incense and scented smoke are all great ways to introduce pleasant aromas into your relaxation shed. Essential oils are also a favourite with spas and therapists alike – certain oils are thought to act on the body's central nervous system, creating a sedating or calming effect. For a relaxing experience, try Roman chamomile, ylang ylang, sandalwood, neroli, clary sage, rose or lavender.

ABOVE **A contemporary pool shed with oversized porthole windows creates a distinctly nautical feel.**
RIGHT **Simple seating echoes the clean lines of the building and the pool.**
OPPOSITE TOP **Natural building materials and simple architecture are in keeping with the surrounding trees and olive groves.**

pool house

Want a shed that's going to make a splash? Two pool houses, high up in the mountains of Provence, prove that aesthetics and practicality don't have to be mutually exclusive.

Can modern architecture sit happily with ancient? The pool houses at Le Jas du Boeuf, France, would suggest that they can, with consummate ease. Nestling on the southern slopes of the Montagne de Lure, in the heart of Haute-Provence, these two über-modern pool houses sit in the grounds of a beautifully restored 200-year-old farmhouse.

The setting is timeless. Halfway between the Alps and the Mediterranean, between the Lure and Luberon mountains and the Durance and Calavon rivers, lies the magical area of the Pays de Forcalquier. All the hallmarks of Provence are there: olive groves, lavender fields, sunflowers, and vineyards heavy with grapes. And, yet, the young owners of this stunning location, Helene Lesur and Luc Beziat, have chosen to build a dazzling 9 x 7m (27 x 21ft) infinity pool, along with two highly

contemporary wooden and glass pool houses, or 'bungalows'. The farmhouse itself is located three kilometres from Cruis, a small village classified as a 'site of character' in the Pays de Forcalquier area. A former stone sheepfold on three hectares of land, it has been innovatively renovated by the owners in an elegant contemporary style.

There are three guest rooms in the house, either en suite or with a private bathroom. They all have their own entrance and either a private terrace or independent access to the grounds. Rough stone and heavy timbers feature heavily in the house, and when it came to building the pool houses it was important to bring in some of the simple elements and natural materials of the house without attempting a pastiche. Past and present meet in concrete, glass, rough metal and Douglas fir.

The pool houses are unashamedly up to date, however, taking inspiration from key elements of modernist architecture. These striking huts contrast beautifully with their ancient surroundings and represent a total departure from the fussy interiors of many period properties – bare white walls, concrete, long stretches of glazing, porthole windows, minimal ornaments, bentwood furniture and simple curtains in natural fibres are all typical of this modernist approach.

Designed as annexes to the main guesthouse, both pool houses face south to afford magnificent views out over the surrounding countryside. Circular windows, both large and small, lend a nautical touch to each pool house. Each one also boasts its own private bathroom, and guests are invited to spend time relaxing at the south-facing infinity swimming pool or in one of

the many secluded corners of the grounds. A simple summer kitchen, with a canvas awning, allows guests to cook in the open air – cooktop, oven, refrigerator, sink – while poolside seating invites you to enjoy your evening meal sitting outside. What better way to while away a summer's evening than sampling local produce – goats' cheeses from Banon, olive oil from Lure and herbal apéritifs from Forcalquier. In the morning, guests wake to a poolside French breakfast – freshly baked croissants and breads from a local boulangerie, local honey and jams, fruit juices, fromage blanc, coffee and tea.

Beautifully simple in both design and execution, the two pool houses are designed to blend in rather than compete with the surrounding countryside. They might be modern in style, but the emphasis on natural materials and decor prevents these smart buildings overshadowing the mature woodland in which they sit.

Large windows and light furnishings give both pool houses a bright, clean feel, softened with natural fabrics and the odd brightly coloured throw. It is a tricky balancing act – organizing a small living space so that it looks both spacious and homely – but one that the owners have managed with great aplomb.

To do this, they used a few simple interior design basics: keeping the spaces clutter-free, creating focal points and using symmetry. Accessories have been kept to a bare minimum – a well-chosen lamp and a simple side table in the bedroom, for

OPPOSITE The soothing neutral decor is lifted and punctuated with a dramatic splash of bright pink.
ABOVE Porthole windows provide ample natural light and frame the view from each guest room.
RIGHT Both pool houses face south so that guests can take in the magnificent views of rural Provence.

example – which helps the space to feel larger than it really is. Our eyes are taken instead to the different focal points around each pool house – the porthole and landscape window frames, and the stunning views beyond. Everything draws our attention away from the interior and focuses it on the breathtaking scenery outside. The buildings create a pleasing symmetry – the notion of 'reflection' runs through them, and not only are the pool houses reflected in the surface of the water, but they mirror each other in style and positioning around the pool as well.

Balance is also achieved through the use of different textures. The hardness of the concrete render is skilfully counterbalanced by the rich solid timber cladding. Inside, the smoothness of the floor surface is balanced by the crisp bedlinen and soft woollen throws. Colour is used cleverly but sparingly. The emphasis is on neutral shades – whites, greys, browns. These provide a gentle backdrop to the natural colours in the landscape, again bringing the attention to the views found outside. Bright, light colours also feel 'clean', an important factor for poolside living, where surfaces are often wet, and dirt can easily be tracked indoors.

Less is definitely more here. Besides, the practicalities of life close to the pool require flooring and furnishings that are simple and hard-wearing. Le Jas du Boeuf proves, however, that practical does not have to mean dull.

LEFT An outdoor kitchen allows guests to eat and entertain by the poolside.
OPPOSITE A cooktop, a Belfast sink and a refrigerator provide everything you need to create an open-air feast.

ABOVE Doors flung wide open allow the sea
air in, while maintaining a cosy space.
RIGHT Compact integral storage is neat and
appealing. The comings and goings of the
tide, as well as the vital grocery list, are
recorded on the miniature blackboard.
OPPOSITE The Sea Shanty's main room is the
hub of family holidays.

seaside retreat

Water lapping through the battered
floorboards and the threat of waves
crashing in may not sound like
everyone's dream holiday. For one
family, however, an old shored-up
houseboat is the ideal haven.

The Skinner family bought the 'Sea Shanty' always intending it
to be a seaside retreat. Their three young children, Bruno, Rollo
and Ludo, spend idyllic Swallows-and-Amazons summers
exploring the rockpools and splashing around in the waves with
their two dogs. And, when the summer season is over, the
family simply closes up the houseboat and become landlubbers
once more for the winter season.

The set-up is basic – no electricity, no running water, no
services – but that's all part of the appeal. Parents Quentin and
Dilly always wanted the family to enjoy the simple pleasures of
seaside life – cricket on the beach, crabbing off the deck,
cockling, shrimping, flotilla expeditions for picnics, and twilight
swims before an easy supper prepared in the tiny kitchen.

The hut has seen many a summer. It has been on its present
site for three-quarters of a century, and previous owners have
had to battle against the elements to prevent the houseboat

from being washed away like a piece of flotsam. Thanks to some serious shoring up with concrete and steel rods, the houseboat can now withstand anything the weather throws at it and is hopefully here to stay.

The interior is wonderfully reminiscent of a 1950s beach holiday – pale blues and ice cream woodwork, nautically themed trinkets, and oars, lifejackets, fishing nets and paddles lashed to the rafters. The Sea Shanty's main room is the focus of family life. A raised seating area opens onto wooden decking and steps leading down to the water – the perfect place for the boys to sit and dip their toes, and for adults to keep a watchful eye while they relax with a book or simply enjoy the view.

Built-in furniture includes a compact kitchenette complete with neat worktops and a large dresser for displaying everyday china, together with a pull-down blackboard that is used for chalking up shopping lists and recording the times of the tides. Two window seats have been fashioned out of reclaimed timber and topped with calico foam cushions and primrose-coloured scatter cushions. The platformed area can be cosily separated from the main living area by simple pale lemon-coloured curtains, to create a comfortable and relaxing area in which to gauge the tide or simply sit and talk. Elsewhere in the space, mismatched furniture creates an informal nautical and rustic air. An antique table, wooden chairs painted in a range of seaside blues, and a waterproof table covering are all practical solutions for a retreat where any precious belongings could easily be damaged by the weather, the saline atmosphere or the constant traipsing in of sand and sea. Nothing of any great value stays in the house, so that the owner's can relax and not worry about leaving their belongings behind at the end of each season.

Off the living area are three bedrooms, allowing the whole family to gather and spend holiday time together. In the main parents' bedroom, a generous amount of storage is neatly provided under the raised bed, while another bedroom houses a fitted bunk bed, with additional storage beneath.

Throughout the house, weatherboarding is used on the interior walls and all the built-in furniture, while slim, plain wooden pelmets frame the windows and uncomplicated curtain headings. The simple floral and plain fabrics were deliberately chosen so that the charming clutter of belongings and the sea view become the dominant focus.

A colour scheme of fresh coastal white on the exterior and pale blue buttermilk indoors is both nautical and engaging, without being kitsch, very much like the retreat itself.

RIGHT A retro cabin bed in pale blue and ice cream paintwork combines a sense of comfort with an air of practicality.

ABOVE All the trademarks of a gypsy wagon: wooden wheels, foldaway front steps and brightly painted balustrades.
RIGHT A compact kitchenette tucks neatly into one end of the caravan.
OPPOSITE This ultimate mobile home is well equipped for guests or holidays.

gypsy caravan

We all yearn to escape from time to time. Gypsy caravans have long held romantic associations with a poetic nomadic lifestyle, free from the cares of workaday life and obligations. A Romany existence journeying gently through the countryside often seems the perfect antidote to the chaos of hectic modern living.

Antique gypsy caravans are hard to come by and often need the skills of specialist restorers to bring them back to their former glory. So what do you do if you want a taste of the travelling life, but have no ancient wagon to hand? Sitting on the edge of a pine forest, this enchanting caravan – or 'roulotte', as it is known by its French creators – is possibly the next best way to grab yourself a shed on the move.

Looking at its chamfered wooden wheels, balustrades, porthole windows and zinc roof, you could be forgiven for thinking that this gypsy caravan has travelled far and wide. But nothing could be further from the truth. This is a roulotte fresh from the workshops of Les Roulottes de Bohème, a group of French artisans who hand-build traditional gypsy caravans for a thoroughly modern market. Perfect for anyone with a bohemian spirit, these circus-coloured gypsy caravans are converted into anything from a home office to a relaxing hideaway. And,

thanks to their very portability, these magical huts can be readily carted off to pastures new whenever the mood for a change of scenery strikes.

But enjoying a travellers rest need not mean giving up all your home comforts. This particular model has been designed to include a fully equipped kitchen with a working hob and sink, together with a bathroom with shower. Sleeping arrangements are cosy and comfortable – at the end of the caravan a double bedroom, with its own porthole window on the world, is neatly partitioned from the living space by a brightly patterned curtain featuring all the colours used in the caravan. Elsewhere, a daybed quickly turns into an extra single bed for night-time. Sheds always demand neat storage, as space is at such a premium, so here doors tucked under the beds lead to unobtrusive drawers and cupboards. A fold-out table means living space can be maximized at night. The colour scheme is gorgeous. Reminiscent of a

ABOVE Bohemian chic in the form of bright primary colours and fabrics in folk designs.
ABOVE RIGHT A tiny treat of a bathroom, complete with working shower, is cleverly shoe-horned into a corner.

OPPOSITE LEFT Showman's colours of yellow and baby blue add to a storybook feel.
OPPOSITE RIGHT A raised double bed behind a full-length curtain provides ample sleeping space at one end of the roulotte.

child's drawing, the lollipop shades of rich lemon yellows, russet browns, cloudy blues and sugar almond pinks add a nostalgic feel to both the inside and exterior of the roulotte.

Delicate floral curtains in acid green and fuchsia pink disguise cooking paraphernalia beneath the painted kitchenette worktop. Red and blue fabrics and painted furniture are crisply set off by a cheerful seaside blue natural matting. And the tiny compact bathroom and bedroom are bathed in baby blue for a relaxing ambience. Keen to continue on this whimsical colour theme, the roulotte is decorated with gloriously clashing cotton fabrics, naïve accessories and cushions piled high. Outside, the window shutters resemble buttons and barge-ware styling, while wagon wheels give the air of pioneers on the move.

Such an inspiring space on wheels, with decor that manages to be both up to date and slightly nostalgic, can only be described as travelling in style.

entertaini

ng spaces

a place to party

From outside dining rooms to barbecue huts, sheds are the ultimate place to wine and dine with friends. They turn everything from impromptu casual get-togethers to formal dinner parties into an occasion to remember.

Whether it is quiet sophistication you want or a place to party, outdoor buildings add an extra dimension to al fresco entertainment and ensure that the weather never spoils your fun. Sheds offer immense flexibility when it comes to outdoor enjoyment; how far you want to take your ideas will depend largely on money, location and planning constraints. But whether you want a simple party shack or a summer kitchen, there are a few factors you need to consider.

Siting your shed as close to the house as possible is a good idea, so that you are not carrying food too great a distance during a meal. Installing lighting and heating in the shed is necessary if you want your guests to linger, while temporary lighting in the form of candles, or lanterns suspended from walls or hung on iron posts in the ground, provides atmosphere as well as illumination. Candles are always an attractive option and, if they contain oils such as citronella or andiroba, will act as a natural bug repellent. Don't be

too quick to switch on any outdoor lights – part of the magic of outdoor dining is allowing our eyes to adjust to the darkness, so that we can enjoy taking in how the natural world looks by candlelight.

Cooking facilities are an important factor. It might sound obvious, but think about the type of cooking you would like to do outside and what kind of facilities you need.

Mediterranean countries have long been used to the idea of having a basic kitchen outside, usually comprising a stone work surface, wood-fired oven and basic sink, and it is not difficult to create your own rustic version. If you want something a bit more sophisticated, outdoor kitchens are fast becoming the must-have garden accessory.

The idea is simple: to bring all the facilities of an indoor kitchen out into the garden. You can create a workspace that not only has a grill or barbecue, but also features kitchen cabinets, sink, taps, island units, rotisserie, dishwasher, refrigerator and freezer.

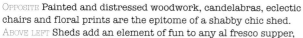

OPPOSITE **Painted and distressed woodwork, candelabras, eclectic chairs and floral prints are the epitome of a shabby chic shed.**
ABOVE LEFT **Sheds add an element of fun to any al fresco supper,** particularly when table linen is themed to tie in with the decor.
ABOVE RIGHT **Be sparing with outdoor lighting when dusk falls. What is appealing by day can take on a whole new atmosphere by candlelight.**

Seating is hugely important when it comes to outdoor entertaining. Your aim should be to create a practical but convivial area in which to welcome friends and visitors. There are many options to consider – from simple wooden benches to sunken dining areas. Wood, stone and metal seating all survive well outside, if properly maintained, and can be softened with removable cushions, bolsters and rugs. If you do choose wood, opt for teak, oak, redwood or cedar, as these tend to survive outside conditions better than pine.

As with the shed itself, all timber should have an FSC mark, ensuring that it has come from a sustainable forest. Painted furniture can be a good way to tie in to an existing decorative scheme or indeed create a strong focal point for your entertaining area. You can also consider creating a 'miniature' seating area for the children, with scaled-down tables and chairs. The huge advantage of entertaining families outdoors is that you do not have to be as concerned about children making a

mess as you maybe would indoors, so you can take a more relaxed approach as to who and how many guests you invite.

Be realistic about how many people you plan to entertain – perhaps just a small table and two chairs would suffice, or do you regularly need to seat large numbers? Flexible foldaway seating or stackable chairs might be useful if you have limited space or you want to store your furniture in the shed. Lightweight furniture is a good idea if you are planning to transport it from indoors or from one part of the garden to another for entertaining. Safetywise, make sure that there is plenty of separation between seating areas and any hot surfaces. You will also need to position tables and chairs away from any cooking smoke if you want to provide a comfortable entertaining space. Give yourself as much space as possible for seating – people tend to expect more room to manoeuvre when they are dining outside. Try not to clutter the space – you don't want guests to be struggling to negotiate their way

OPPOSITE AND RIGHT An interesting mix of
natural materials, soft textures and pale
colours, teamed with simple cream crockery
(right), lends an air of faded elegance to this
waterside supper.

around plant pots and garden tools, or freestanding lighting, especially
if they are carrying drinks or plates of food.

Wipe-clean oilcloths make appealing and useful table coverings,
while matching seat cushions and tablecloth will create a unified look.
If you are going to eat beneath an awning or canopy, it can be an
effective decorating tactic to tie in your choice of fabrics to suit the
occasion – formal or relaxed, celebratory or everyday.

EATING OUTDOORS

It can be a real inconvenience moving furniture and guests if the
weather suddenly decides to change. Prepare for all eventualities. The
perfect dining or party shed will be able to adapt to different weather
conditions; awnings, sails and canopies can provide shelter from both
rain and sunshine if you plan to eat outside, while blinds or voile
curtains will shade anyone sitting inside. There's no reason that you

cannot use your shed as a year-round party or dining venue. Just make
sure that the building is well insulated and comfortable during the
winter months. Guests tend to dress in particularly light clothing –
going for the party look, rather than practicality – so you might need to
provide extra heating to keep everyone happy. A wood-burning stove is
a popular option in party sheds. It not only throws out a considerable
amount of heat, but also provides an inviting ambience.

If you plan to entertain outside on a regular basis, your shed will
need an area of hard surfacing. Guests can soon make a mess of a
neatly groomed lawn, and wet grass is a real slipping hazard. Stone
flags or wooden decking will provide a practical, even surface for table
and chairs, and, unlike lawns, will soon dry off when the sunshine
returns. Just be sure to coat any stone or timber flooring with an anti-
slip finish, as it can become mouldy, and seal it to prevent food and
drink spills staining the floor of your shed.

LEFT Wood is always a solid choice for garden furniture – remember that hardwoods tend to be more durable and longer lasting than softwoods.
OPPOSITE Timber decking creates an instant entertaining area, complete with table, chairs, deck chairs and hammock.

Fragrant plants can really enhance the experience of outdoor entertaining. Herbs are the perfect choice: they smell fantastic and also double up as outdoor store-cupboard ingredients for your cooking. Certain fragrant plants release their wonderful scent only in the evening; honeysuckle, moonflower, jasmine, tuberose and evening primrose are just a few. Position them along walkways or around seating areas, so that guests can brush past them. Some perfumed plants, such as clematis and sweet pea, are also climbers, and these can be trained up and around the shed for maximum effect.

LOCATION, LOCATION

There is no greater luxury than being able to construct a shed for entertaining in the perfect spot. If, however, you have to take into account certain constraints – such as an open-plan garden or the effect on nearby neighbours; not to mention unpredictable weather – there are ways to accommodate these sometimes limiting factors.

Nothing spoils a party more quickly than an irate neighbour. Without sounding too much like a party pooper, you also need to consider how your shed will affect the surrounding houses.

Every year, councils receive thousands of complaints from people affected by noise from neighbours' outdoor parties and barbecues. You will need to think about where your shed will cause least nuisance when it is buzzing with guests. Consider soundproofing the shed to reduce the amount noise of that escapes. When you are planning your shed, think about sound-insulating materials. Plasterboard is generally quite good at cutting down the transmission of airborne sounds such as speech and music, but it is worth investing in high-performance plasterboards, such as Gyproc SoundBloc, which are specially designed to provide excellent insulation against noise.

The position of your shed can also help. If your shed is going to have French windows or an outside seating area, place those on the side of the shed furthest away from your neighbours. The bulk of the shed will act as a natural sound barrier and mask a good proportion of the noise. Being neighbourly will also go a long way – if you are planning a shed party, your neighbours are likely to be much more understanding if you keep them updated or even invite them to join you. Keep the music volume at a suitable level, reducing it as the evening goes on, and make sure that everyone leaves quietly when the fun has finished.

LEFT Through late spring and summer, family and friends spill over into the tent sitting in the grounds of Christina Strutt's country home.
ABOVE This ever-changing temporary shelter provides an inspiring showcase for Christina's exquisite fabrics.

country feast

Since when are sheds only for men? Christina Strutt, owner of Cabbages & Roses, which specializes in vintage-print fabrics and homewares, created an unashamedly romantic and nostalgic entertaining space, with a surprising twist.

Some of the best things in life are fleeting. The inspiration for this temporary shed came about after a birthday party, when owner Christina Strutt, the brains behind Cabbages & Roses, hired a marquee. Feeling so sad when it was returned, she decided to have a permanent one made for the space.

Living in an historic home, Christina found it impossible to get planning permission to extend the house. Owners of listed or historically significant or heritage buildings, and people who live in conservation areas, tend to find it more difficult to make external changes to their properties, and even a traditional shed may have needed special permission.

Christina needed to find a way around the strict planning rules, and instead cleverly came up with the idea of a temporary structure. Making the most of the somewhat fickle English weather, the tent is in use from April to September, fully furnished with dining table, sofas and a bed for afternoon naps, or for teenage guests to colonize when the house is full.

Its purpose is to enlarge the house in the warmer months, providing much-needed space for a busy family. Friends and relatives feast under its canopy, shelter from the rain and even, on the odd occasion, hide from the sun. The sides of the tent can be rolled up or left down, depending on the weather or the event. It also doubles as the perfect working space and party room, and makes an ideal spot for photo shoots, providing an instant backdrop for any setting, whether it's a bedroom, a tent, a lunch party or a tea party.

By decorating the tent with romantic fabrics and flea-market finds, Christina has created the epitome of contemporary country style, without it costing the earth. Christina describes her company's vintage style as a 'celebration of the handmade' – all her products are individually handcrafted and the linens are handprinted. Her love of time-honoured crafts and simple old-fashioned sewing are truly reflected in this simple space.

With so many beautiful vintage designs to choose from, the tent is always furnished in the latest Cabbages & Roses creations and makes a perfect foil for Christina's fabrics and furniture. Favourite family pieces also make a splash: the wirework candle chandelier was a present to Christina's husband, the garden furniture inherited from her mother-in-law and the Welsh rugs a gift from an old friend.

Thanks to the temporary nature of the structure, Christina never gets a chance to tire of her tent. When the mood strikes, she can completely change the furnishings – which she often does, about three or four times a season.

RIGHT Delicate ironwork chairs, sea-grass flooring and a tented canopy are reminiscent of a garden party marquee, the original inspiration for Christina's design.

ABOVE AND RIGHT This basic black box is deceptive. French windows and a canopy conceal a stunning dining room.
OPPOSITE An opulent chandelier and mirror contrast beautifully with a flawless interior.

dine in style

An ingenious and discreet London shed opens out, jack-in-a-box style, to reveal an astonishingly simple but elegant cedar-clad dining space that is compact but still inviting.

Fancy supper in a shed? Most of us would not automatically link gourmet dining and garden huts, but this seemingly unlikely invitation is one you would be crazy to refuse. Built by London company Square Feet Architects, this outbuilding has far more to it than initially meets the eye.

At first glance, the shed looks like a sleek but simple seaside beach hut, stained black so that it merges with the urban landscape. Timber in construction and sitting on a raised solid base, this looks like a shed with nothing to hide. And yet ...

The surprise here – and the shed's true nature – lies on the inside. Open the double doors, and you are instantly hit with a bold, beautiful and totally unexpected interior. This is a dining-room annexe with a difference.

Walls, floor and ceiling are clad, top to toe, in the warm rich tones of cedar. This wood is not only exquisite to look at and naturally perfumed, but also has a tight grain, making it highly

durable and an excellent practical choice for outbuildings. Cedar has also long been used for its rot-resistant and insect-repelling qualities – properties that stand any shed in good stead. When choosing cedar, however, it is important to make sure that it comes from a sustainable source. Cedar comes mainly from two places: the United States and Brazil. In both countries, irresponsible logging is destroying the natural ecosystem and threatening the habitats of many important species. If you are going to buy cedar, always ensure that it is FSC-certified.

Back inside the shed, the furnishings are spare but elegant. Square footage, as with most sheds, is at a premium, so some simple but clever design tricks maximize the feeling of space. A transparent glass table prevents the tiny space from feeling cramped, while a large rococo mirror bounces light around the room and adds a playful touch to an otherwise pared-down scheme. Mix-and-match antique dining chairs in a darker wood and a sparkly vintage chandelier also humanize the space and give the shed more than a hint of old-school glamour.

At the back of the space, a black ceramic-clad recess draws our attention. This little alcove makes an ingenious design statement, inviting us to explore further into the space. It also hides the wood-burning stove – a much-needed source of heat for any late-night dinner parties.

A wood-burning stove is a clever choice for such a small space. Even the tiniest stove will belt out a generous amount of heat, which is plenty enough for a small dining annexe. It also prevents the need of having to go through the hassle of getting connected to a mains source of fossil fuel. The architects at Square Feet also included an electrical supply for the lighting and power points in the plans – essential if this shed is to be anything more than just a daytime space.

The main house is only a stone's throw away, preventing diners from feeling too isolated and allowing the shed to feel part of the bigger picture. It is an obvious advantage, too, that food and drink can be easily transported from the kitchen to the dining table, without the risk of food cooling off on the journey.

On a warm summer's evening, the shed's double doors remain open, and guests are sheltered by a wooden canopy. When the party is over and all that is left is to clear away the dishes, everything simply folds away, quickly returning the shed to its witty disguise.

This is a shed that fully reflects the architect's philosophy and approach to design – young, dynamic and innovative, but also deeply down to earth.

guest

rooms

annexes & guest rooms

Building a shed as a guest annexe for all those visiting friends and family is the ideal solution for creating more space without breaking the budget.

ABOVE When situated independently from the main house, your visitors can come and go as they please.
OPPOSITE A pargeted porch and a picket fence reinforce a sense of separation and privacy for this self-contained guest cabin.

It can be a real squeeze fitting friends and family into your existing accommodation when they come to stay, whether they descend on you for a weekend or weeks.

Few of us can afford houses with rooms that are kept permanently empty for the few times when visitors sleep over. Creating a guest room at the bottom of the garden has turned out to be the perfect answer for many families pushed for space. It is also fantastic for guests, who can enjoy peace, quiet and privacy away from the main house.

If you need something more permanent, it is also possible to convert a shed into a granny annexe to offer year-round accommodation. Elderly relatives (and in some cases adult children) appreciate the sense of independence that a granny annexe offers, while feeling secure that company and help are only a few metres away in the main house. Turning a shed into sleeping accommodation needs careful thought, and more facilities than a workshop or office.

Some sheds don't require planning permission. When you start to put sleeping accommodation into a shed, however, or plan for it to be occupied on a regular basis as a granny flat or holiday let, you are moving firmly into the realm of planning approval and compliance with building regulations. Factors such as fire safety, insulation, electrical installation and drainage will all need to comply with strict building codes to ensure the health and safety of the shed's occupants, permanent or otherwise.

In terms of difficulty, getting permission for temporary accommodation (i.e. a guest room) is more straightforward than attempting to house someone permanently at the end of your garden. It is sometimes easier to get permission if you can prove that the occupant is a close relative and the shed will never be sold separately from the main house, but a quick chat with the planning department will soon tell you whether it is feasible or not. A shed granny annexe is,

ABOVE, BELOW AND OPPOSITE **This lakeside retreat boasts everything visitors could need for a self-contained summer break, including an ingenious outdoor shower for a refreshing blast of cold water.**

more often than not, self-contained, as opposed to an extension, which means that it is subject to different planning rules. If the shed already exists, you may also have to apply for 'change of use' from non-domestic to domestic use. Your local planning officer can tell you more about what to do if this applies.

The process does not stop there. Once you have established that it is possible to create your annexe, you will have to ensure that any building work complies with building regulations. The building control officer at your local council will be able to guide you through this process and inspect any alterations.

SEASONAL OR YEAR-ROUND?

One of the first decisions that you will need to make is what time of the year you plan to use the shed for guest accommodation. If it is just for summer use, the shed can be a much simpler structure than a building intended for year-round occupation. Teenagers, for example, may love

the idea of a rustic outdoor space where friends can crash after a barbecue on balmy evenings. This kind of space is essentially a wooden tent and needs very little in terms of facilities; all it offers is shelter from the elements, good ventilation so that it is not stuffy and airless, and a flat surface on which to sleep.

To keep your guests comfortable during the cooler and wetter months of the year, however, you will need to provide generous insulation, draught-proofing, heating and damp-proof measures. The shed will need to feel as comfortable and warm as a room in the main house – especially if your guests are elderly relatives or young families

with children. See the Making Space chapter (page 184) for details on how to make a shed into a cosy, liveable space, whatever the weather.

When you are creating a guest space, it is really important to think about how your guests will use the space in your absence. The best guest rooms are those which are as appealing and luxurious as a boutique hotel, but also practical. A guest shed needs to be clear of clutter, leaving your guests to make their mark on the space. You can decorate the space to make it homely, but be careful not to make it too personal – you don't want your guests to feel as if they are intruding. Very valuable or sentimental items are also best left in the main house

OPPOSITE **A converted railway carriage makes a spacious and cosy crash pad and a welcome retreat at the end of a garden.**

BELOW **Guest rooms need to be inviting and clutter-free, allowing guests to feel instantly relaxed and at home, with room to move.**

RIGHT, BELOW AND OPPOSITE **Wall-to-wall timber gives these guest bedrooms a sense of instant warmth, whether in a smart mountain cabin in Colorado designed by Ron Mason (right and opposite) or a traditional log cabin in New Mexico (below).**

in case of a break-in or accidental damage. A visitors' book is a fun addition to the space, and guests will spend many a happy hour adding their thoughts and looking through the comments of previous visitors.

COMFORTABLE BEDS

Bedwise, invest in a good-quality frame and mattress for your guests – it's vital that they get a good night's rest. Make up the bed(s) with clean ironed cotton or linen sheets, and include at least two pillows per person (you can keep extra pillows in the wardrobe). It can be difficult to predict how warm or cool your guests like to be when sleeping, so include a good selection of heavy and llight blankets to cover all eventualities. A hot-water bottle, occasional throw or electric blanket might also go down well in the cooler months.

STORAGE

Depending on how often you plan to have guests, you may want to use the shed for other purposes than a bedroom. If your guest room isn't going to be solely a guest room, you will need to think about where to store your belongings when you have company. If you cannot face

moving everything out of the shed every time you have visitors, create generous underbed storage or a dedicated cupboard, rather than making your guests sleep in a room littered with spare belongings. In addition to storage for your things, you will need to provide somewhere for guests to put their belongings for the duration of their stay. A set of bedside drawers is ideal for small items, while a wardrobe or fitted cupboard is essential for clothes and luggage. Plentiful hangers and a hanging canvas shoe bag will also help to keep this small space as tidy as possible. A collapsible luggage rack is a handy addition, so that guests have somewhere apart from the bed to put their suitcase while they are unpacking when they arrive, and repacking when they leave.

ABOVE LEFT, ABOVE RIGHT AND OPPOSITE **A shed of contrasts. The strikingly dark timber cladding hides a light-filled interior dressed with antique and 20th-century furniture.**

WELCOMING TOUCHES

A coat stand, full-length mirror, iron, ironing board, reading lamp and alarm clock are guest-room essentials and can easily be tucked away in the wardrobe when not in use. It might also be worth including a portable television, DVD player and a stack of books and magazines, so that guests can amuse themselves if either they or you need time out. Visitors will also need a relaxing place to sit; depending on the space available, a small sofa or armchair will give your guests an extra space in which to put their feet up.

It is a real treat to leave your guests a tray of goodies, such as hot drinks and cake or biscuits, especially if they have had a long journey. Fresh flowers picked from the garden and a newspaper with details of local events also provide a perfect welcome and a personal touch.

BATHROOM SPACE

A guest room really needs to be self-contained. An en-suite bathroom or shower room is a must, as most guests will not relish the thought of stumbling up the garden to use the bathroom, especially during the night. The en-suite does not have to be huge – a toilet and cloakroom hand basin can easily fit into a space of little more than 1.5 square metres (16 square feet). If you want to include a shower room, the space will need to be bigger, but you can still easily accommodate a shower, standard basin and toilet into an area 2.5 metres (8 feet) long by 1 metre (about 3 feet) wide. The bathroom will need its own sources of lighting and heat, both of which need to be considered properly at the planning stage. Think, too, about whether you are going to create a separate room or whether the bathroom area can be screened off with a curtain or else form a part of the overall living space, perhaps separated by a half-height wall. Another option is to add on a bathroom to an existing shed by creating a lean-to extension.

As with any guest room, the bathroom in your guest shed will need to be well stocked with toilet tissue and other personal care items. It

ABOVE LEFT, ABOVE RIGHT AND RIGHT **Somewhere to freshen up: a small cloakroom suite complete with toilet, hand basin and shower will provide guests with everything they need in a compact guest annexe.** OPPOSITE **A simple kitchenette is an essential element for those long-stay friends and family.**

is always a welcoming gesture to include new toothbrushes and toothpaste in case guests have forgotten theirs, as well as soap, a hair dryer and unopened bottles of shampoo and conditioner. Fresh towels are absolutely essential – most hotels usually work on the basis of one large towel, one hand towel and one facecloth per person.

Keep the overall decor of your bathroom simple, to match both the proportions and style of your shed. Simple plain tiling or tongue-and-groove panelling work best in a garden building inspired by the country. For an urban or eco feel, use water-resistant plywood to provide a modernist twist to bath and sink panelling.

KITCHEN SPACE

For a shed that is going to be occupied on a permanent basis, or if you are planning to hire out your shed as bed-and-breakfast holiday accommodation, you will almost certainly need to install cooking facilities. A basic kitchenette needs only to include a sink, a refrigerator and a two-ring hob, plus some areas for food preparation. This could be in the form of either a fitted worktop or a pull-down tabletop if space is limited. A microwave and an oven are optional, but you will need to provide a cupboard with some basic equipment, including pots and pans, crockery, glassware, cutlery and utensils. To supplement a basic kitchenette, make the most of your outside space and think about a chiminea or barbecue area, and create an outdoor kitchen to complement the basic facilities provided indoors.

If you cannot splash out on installing a kitchenette in your guest room, it is still important to include the wherewithal for guests to make themselves a drink. A kettle, mugs, tea, coffee, sugar and a mini-fridge with milk are standard – even better if you include a welcoming bottle of wine too.

ABOVE Antique shoe lasts add a whimsical
note to this circus carriage.
RIGHT A delightful modern interpretation
of a Victorian showman's wagon.
OPPOSITE Easy elegance ensues from this
combination of monochromatic fabrics with
stately rosewood furniture.

the carriage

A contemporary version of a
Victorian showman's wagon, this
compact cabin has become a favourite
bolt hole for family and friends alike –
and is sure to appeal to anyone who
ever had dreams of running away
to join the circus ...

When the circus came to town, Felicity Loudon had one of her
best ideas yet. Inspired by a showman's caravan, she set about
creating her own take on a travellers rest.

Named after the town where they were first made, Felicity's
Reading wagon is beautifully simple. Five metres (15 feet) long,
the wooden cabin is built around an ex-military chassis, allowing
it to be towed around the grounds of her home in Pusey,
Oxfordshire, as the mood takes her.

Depending on the time of year, guests may find themselves
a stone's throw from the house or tucked away in the orchard.
'The fact that it is mobile means that I can put it in different
locations during the year,' she explains. 'In the spring it's nice to
be in the orchard, and in the summer by the lake or a cornfield,
but during the autumn it needs to be stationed close to the
house, so that the light and heating can be plugged in to the
mains electricity of the house.'

ABOVE The lozenge window in the stable-style door lets in light without sacrificing guests' privacy.
RIGHT Full-height ticking curtains draw to reveal a compact but functional kitchenette.

But roughing it this is not. High-gloss wooden panelling and a corrugated tin roof keep the elements at bay, while a generator and water tank provide guests with all the power and water they need. On balmy summer evenings, visitors are also encouraged to enjoy a slice of showman life and dine outside, warmed by a roaring log fire.

Inside, Felicity has decked out the carriage in a crisp, campaign-style decor – black-and-white ticking for the walls and blinds, black carpet and genteel rosewood furniture. Guests curl up in a raised bed with monogrammed linen sheets, cashmere blankets and faux-fur throws – many from her immaculate collection at the Private House. This is English style at its best – restrained, but reassuringly luxurious. Much of the carriage's charm lies in its decoration, especially the proliferation of well-chosen accessories, a feature that would not be lost on Romany

ABOVE High-gloss black paint is an authentic
finish for traditional carriages.
RIGHT White tongue-and-groove panelling
provides a seamless, practical backdrop for
a ceramic sink, enamel stove and worktop.

travellers. Historically, when gypsies
stopped overnight, they would unpack
all their pictures, ornaments and special
possessions, and put them on display.
Come morning, they would pack it all up
again, and move on.

Back in the carriage, floor-to-ceiling
ticking curtains separate the sleeping
area from a pretty kitchenette, complete
with tongue-and-groove panelling,
Belfast sink, enamel stove and bespoke
fitted cupboards.

Felicity's carriage has been such a
success that she has started custom
building 'Retreats' for her clients. All
sorts of combinations are possible –
bedroom, kitchen, study, even a mini
casino. As the ultimate present for the
person with everything, the Retreat can
be fitted out to suit diverse interests,
wishes and dreams. Some are panelled;
some have fabric walls; some are for
work; others for play. They even come in
every colour … as long it's black.

ABOVE **Windows on all four sides of the tree house give guests panoramic views of the surrounding treetops.**
RIGHT **The balcony, constructed from locally sourced timber, blends neatly into the surrounding woodland.**
OPPOSITE **Autumn tones of striped wood, leaf green and warm orange extend indoors.**

woodland retreat

If you want to stay at Todd Oldham's house, you need a head for heights. Todd is a designer famous for his fresh, unpretentious and often humorous approach, so it should come as no surprise that his guest accommodation is something a little out of the ordinary.

Perched almost 20 metres (60 feet) in the sky, nestling among five huge trees, sits a wooden cabin, accessible only by winding flights of wooden steps. On the side of a hill to hide from the prevailing winds, this tree-dweller's paradise serves as the perfect guest room, clubhouse, design studio and nature-watching perch. In fact, according to Todd, anyone that pops round to visit almost invariably ends up in the treetops.

Creating this sky-high shed came with its own set of practical challenges. The form emerged from its functional requirements: the lightest of materials had to be used in its construction, from wooden panelling to bead boards, twelve shades of hand-dyed corduroy and back-painted glass. The views are magnificent. To make the most of them, windows have been fitted on all four faces of the tree house, giving a 360-degree sweep of the forest. A narrow balcony also makes a great viewing platform – the ideal spot for a tree-top supper or for simply chilling out.

Left Metal door handles in twig shapes echo real wood elsewhere in the room.
Above Modernism meets handmade style in the living area.
Opposite A mezzanine bunk-bed sleeping area frees up the floor space below.

The installation of electricity and heating keeps guests cosy in the cooler months and, with the practicalities taken care of, Todd could really have some fun with the interior. To maximize the available space, a mezzanine floor provides an area for sleeping and leaves the ground floor free to accommodate a large seating area, and ample fitted storage throughout is made from locally sourced timber, while birch branches are used for the bunk-bed railings.

The handmade-meets-modern aesthetic can be found on the the walls, where every few stripes of wooden panelling are painted varying shades, sheens and tones. This gives richness and depth to the otherwise flat panelling – and a whimsical feel reminiscent of a child's hideaway. The playful design continues throughout – naive paintings, rustic ladders, cheerful mobiles, bright cushions and quirky accessories make this a colourful, adventurous space. Just remember not to look down too often.

ABOVE A compact kitchen comprises rustic worktop, white crockery and slick storage.
RIGHT Karin has lifted any large expanses of white with a striking tomato red fabric.
OPPOSITE In summer, guests spill over into the garden from the raised dining area.

friends to stay

When space is at a premium, storage becomes a top priority. Here, in this Swedish summer house, one architect has combined clever space-saving solutions with all the comfort and charm of a Scandinavian guesthouse.

Karin Stenqvist spent many a happy hour designing her guesthouse. Working with her husband, Oscar, she built ten different scale models of the summer house, experimenting with different room layouts and furniture.

The result is a delight, complete with a balcony as a perfect space for drinks and dining with loved ones. A large home-made dining table is plenty big enough to seat a convivial gathering – wooden chairs on one side and built-in seating on the other. Karin was keen to make the most of the space, so the bench also doubles as a handy storage space, while chairs are hung on the windbreak wall when not in use.

Inside, the attention to detail continues. Useful storage is everywhere. High-up shelving, fitted wardrobes, underbed storage, hanging rails, wooden boxes on wheels – all control clutter and keep the house functioning as a guest space. And the compact kitchen is a godsend in gloomy weather.

playho

uses

childhood games

For generations, parents have grasped the importance of letting their children play outdoors. Many a happy childhood has been spent in a secret den at the bottom of the garden, a playhouse shed or a fantasy tree house above it all.

OPPOSITE This pint-sized summer house is a fantastic shelter for children and a stimulus for imaginative play.
ABOVE RIGHT A playhouse, perched in the branches of a majestic copper beech tree, allows older children to have treetop tea parties and sleepovers.

Running, jumping, building, climbing and even falling over are all childhood activities that are part of becoming a physically confident adult – fun for the outdoors and fun in children's playhouses. Active children keep fit from racing around outdoors, using parts of their bodies that might not always be fully exercised by indoor play.

Any playhouse you choose will have to withstand the rigours of childhood play. It is also vital that the materials do not pose a safety hazard to your child. Timber is a naturally splintery material, and you won't be able to avoid these entirely, but you should always check that any wood is strong and durable, and conforms to national standards for children's play equipment. Wood should be exterior grade and treated with a child-safe preservative. All metal fixings should be free of any sharp edges and galvanized to prevent rust. Any windows must be toughened, whether it's toughened glass or safety Perspex. Children are notorious for

trapping fingers, so ask for safety or 'no-trap' hinges to be fitted on all openings, including doors and windows.

Children fall over. It's a fact of life. Even if the playhouse is designed for ground level (i.e. not raised), you still need to ensure that the surrounding surfaces are soft enough to take the impact of a child's fall and minimize injury. If the playhouse is designed to be elevated – for example, a tree house or a playhouse with a balcony – it is absolutely essential to get the ground surface right.

Children need different things at different times of their life. Playhouses in all their forms need to be designed with your child's (or children's) age and abilities in mind. It can be difficult to make a judgement about this, so it can be helpful to take inspiration from the safety guidelines that are applied to public and school playgrounds.

Any playhouse must be appropriate to a child's age and maturity level. Playground equipment is usually divided into two age

groups: two- to five-year-olds and five- to twelve-year-olds. Children in the older age category are much more physically adept than preschoolers and can cope with more sophisticated, larger play equipment.

FANTASY SHEDS

Children's outdoor play is a very sociable activity, as children can be noisier and more boisterous than they are indoors, without fear of adult intervention. Outdoor play is also more independent. Children still need supervision, but outdoor play tends to receive less direction from grown-ups. Kids learn to make decisions without being prompted; they set the agenda, take a few risks and discover things for themselves.

Outdoor play feels different from indoor play. Textures, sounds and smells are different. Children can interact with trees, flowers, insects and animals in their natural habitat. The outside is a wonderfully unsanitized environment too. Kids inevitably get covered in water and mud, especially if the weather turns and the heavens open.

This and facing page Playhouses give children the freedom to play, learn and dream through make-believe, whether it is in a chocolate-box cottage (opposite top left), miniature Tudor house (opposite top right), pirate shed (left), timber-frame woodman's cottage (below) or gypsy caravan (opposite bottom).

Your children will probably make their own drama, but you can also encourage their imagination with a few props for the playhouse. Dressing-up costumes and old clothes are always great fun and are an easy way to start off role-play activities. Large sheets and blankets can be used as a tablecloth for a teddy bear's picnic or a pirate's sail. Playing 'house' is a favourite activity for Wendy or toy houses, so your little

Outdoor play really fires the imagination. Children love to role-play. Playhouses in all their forms – whether a sturdy wooden tree house, a self-contained gypsy caravan, a mock Tudor playshed or a simple home-made den – give children the opportunity to act out different characters and scenarios. Tree houses become cowboy strongholds or a pirate ship; Wendy houses and cubby houses are transformed into a fairy palace or a dainty tea room. As adults, the best thing we can do is to provide a stimulating and safe environment for our children to play.

Surfaces are important, and some are more suitable than others. Concrete, stone slabs, tarmac and similar hard surfaces are unsafe. Grass and soil, which are common options for most gardens, are also not ideal, as they can become hard-packed through use and weathering. Wood chips, mulch, sand, pea gravel or shredded rubber are the best options, and should be loose-filled to a depth of 30 centimetres (12 inches) for any equipment up to 2.5 metres (8 feet) high. Even then, guardrails should be used.

LEFT AND OPPOSITE A traditional showman's caravan delights children of all ages, while providing enough room for work, rest and play.
BELOW A more colourful take on a circus carriage, with its big-top stripes and strong purples.

ones may love a set of plastic teacups and plates, or a pretend kitchen. Cardboard boxes also have endless uses in make-believe play, from a train carriage to a hat.

HOME FROM HOME

While you may want to have a say in the external decoration of the playhouse, your children will relish the opportunity to put their stamp on the inside. Let them choose the wall colour for the inside – they may even want to help you paint. Children gravitate towards brighter, cheerful colours, and as adults we sometimes become too fixated on what is tasteful rather than what will appeal to kids. Your children may want to show off their creative talents and paint a mural or hang some of their own artwork on the walls. Perhaps they have some favourite posters? An old rug or carpet remnant will soften the floor and make it feel more like a house, as will simple curtains or blinds. Quick curtains can be created by stitching a hem or tabs along the top of two gingham tea towels and hanging them on a thin curtain rod. Little tiebacks will help to keep them out of the way.

A miniature table and chairs is a lovely addition to a playhouse and can be painted to match the decor of the interior. If your budget is tight, car-boot sales, garage sales or on-line auctions are a great way to pick up second-hand bargains – children grow so quickly that most items receive very little wear and tear before they are passed on. Just check that any furniture is well made, sturdy and free of damage. Look out for bookcases, beanbags, toy boxes and other useful pieces to help kit out the playroom.

When children are lucky enough to have their own sleepover den in which to have friends over to stay, they really can have free rein to create their own mini home-from-home, complete with sleeping space. Bunk beds are perennially popular with children from the age of five upwards. There is something fun and romantic attached to having to climb up or around the stairs to bed, and adults always seem to retain vivid childhood memories of sleeping in bunk beds. Whether freestanding, fitted or custom-made, these can double up as units with additional storage or else as informal daybeds. Paint them to match the wall colour, to enhance the sense of space.

Remember to include shelving for storing and displaying books and games. Coat hooks and peg rails are useful for hanging up coats, and a wooden box or bench with a lift-up lid is a good idea for storing shoes, blankets or spare clothes.

Flooring is best kept simple and safe. Make sure that rugs are shored up with a non-slip underlay, while bare floorboards or plywood floors look good painted and varnished to protect them.

LEFT Children's playhouses don't have to be cluttered. Clever storage and simple styling keep this sleepover space light and airy. OPPOSITE An ingeniously simple take on bunk beds leaves more space for play.

ABOVE Time for tea. Yves Taralon's great-nieces and great-nephews organize a teddy bears' picnic.
RIGHT Pretty fabrics and practical storage add to this magical Wendy house.
OPPOSITE A fairytale miniature house comes complete with wooden shutters, a thatched roof and child-sized furniture.

kids' space

The term 'Wendy house' was first coined a hundred years ago, after Wendy in J M Barrie's much-loved Peter Pan stories. More than a century later, one French designer has re-created his own storybook version, complete with thatched roof and tiny wooden shutters.

Tucked away at the bottom of a rambling orchard sits a fairytale playhouse. Here, the young kith and kin of one of France's top designers organize teddy bears' picnics, share stories and let their imaginations truly fly. Created by decorator and artistic director of Hermès, Yves Taralon, for his great-nieces and great-nephews, this tiny thatched cottage is the focus of endless creative play and make-believe. Known affectionately as 'Uncle Gateaux' by his family, Yves has constructed a world straight from the pages of a storybook.

Standing just a few metres high, this small toy house provides endless hours of fun and an opportunity for the children to immerse themselves in a world of their own. The rustic architectural details add to the illusion – fretwork fascia boards, straw roof, ledge and brace door, metal letter box and working shutters. You could be forgiven for thinking that Goldilocks might just make an appearance. Everything is re-created in

perfect miniature. Tables, chairs, doors and beds are all charmingly child-sized, helping to inspire little imaginations and keep grown-ups away.

Sunlight pours in through casement windows on either side of the little front door, boosted with light from portholes in the gables. When the shutters are closed, light peeps through the cutout shapes – heart, diamond, club and spade – motifs taken from every child's favourite, playing cards.

But it is not just a house for looking at. Thanks to its robust construction, this is a playhouse designed for fun. The interior is clad top to bottom with thick timber planks – a tough and durable surface able to withstand the constant trampling of muddy wellies and exuberant play. Sunlight pours in through casement windows on either side of the little front door, boosted with light from portholes in the gables.

Inside the playhouse, double bunk beds and thick quilts provide cosy accommodation for sleepovers, with handy underbed storage and shelves to keep toys and games safely stowed. A fold-down desk and simple stool make an excellent impromptu working space for when the rain threatens play.

But this playhouse really comes into its element on long summer days. What better way for children to while away their time than sitting in dappled shade on their very own veranda, presiding over a teddy bears' picnic, complete with miniature tables, chairs and a wooden cooker?

LEFT Double bunk beds provide plenty of room for sleepovers.
OPPOSITE Chunky shelves and storage boxes keep the children's toys together and the small space free from clutter.

MAKING SPACE

As with any building project, large or small, the key to creating the perfect shed is to work out exactly what it will be used for. Only when you have defined your shed's purpose can you really set about the planning stage. The best approach is to sit down with a pen and paper, and ask yourself some basic questions about what you want in terms of materials, style, design, cost and function.

RIGHT Artist Malcolm Temple's shed is a study in creating an interesting new shed from reclaimed materials and to a tight budget.

planning your shed

Whether designing a new shed from scratch, decorating and choosing furniture for an off-the-shelf shed or refitting a potting shed, planning ahead will save you both time and money.

The success of any project depends on the quality of the brief – a well thought-out plan will save you time, money and hassle further down the line. It also gives you the best chance of producing a shed that is not only functional and practical, but aesthetically pleasing too. So exactly what questions do you need to ask yourself?

If you employ an architect, they will work with you, the client, to go through a planning process. The end result will be your 'brief' – it might not be intended to be seen by anyone but you, but you should always remember that the success of any project ultimately depends

on the quality of the brief. So take the time to make sure that it is well considered and fulfils its role.

WHAT IS THE SHED FOR?
It might seem a no-brainer, but you need to be clear about your reasons for embarking on this project. What do you intend to do with the space? Is it for work or pleasure? Is it for noisy or quiet activities? Is it going to be a home office or a gym? A music room or a guest suite? Treat your shed as if it were a space in your house – it may be at the end of the garden, but that's no reason for it not to benefit from all the home comforts.

OPPOSITE Planning the size, location and building budget for your shed will help you to develop a design brief for an architect or clarify your own ideas.
ABOVE RIGHT Think carefully about where to locate your shed and what architectural style will suit your house and your garden.

Sheds can be functional, luxurious, sociable, quirky, practical, creative – any number of things. Each of these spaces will demand different requirements in terms of location, size, number of rooms, facilities, storage and furnishings. You may want to focus on one function or create a dual-purpose space. If you want the shed for a clearly defined domestic purpose, but still think you may need extra outside storage, think about supplementing the shed with an add-on such as a log store or a lean-to for housing any firewood, compost bins or garden tools. Consider the possibility of placing two sheds side by side, as long as they are not allowed to dominate and overwhelm the garden.

WHO WILL USE THE SHED?

Will it be a small, private space or something for family and friends to enjoy too? The use of the shed may change with time and life events such as retirement or children growing up. Does the space need to be child-friendly or suitable for people with mobility problems? Is it a space intended for visitors and guests? Consult the views of anyone else who will want to use the space – you might be surprised to hear another person's take on the project.

If you are planning to spend a substantial amount of money on this project, it's definitely worth thinking about how the use of the shed will change over time. You may only want the shed for occasional events at the moment, for example; however, as family life grows and changes, could it be adapted for more regular use? Is it a good idea to install electricity, water and insulation now, even if you don't immediately plan to use them? 'Future-proofing' the shed at this stage will save time and money later on when you want to change or expand its purpose.

WHAT FACILITIES WILL THE SHED NEED?

This question can be answered only when you have decided on the function of the shed. You may decide that you only want to use your shed in the summer, during daylight hours, and therefore do not need additional power or services. To make the most from your shed all year round, however, it is well worth getting connected so you can be self-contained. Most sheds will need electricity, but think about whether you need water and drainage for kitchen, workshop or bathroom facilities.

If you are planning to work from your shed, get quotations for installing phone and Internet facilities. A telephone engineer can easily install a separate dedicated phone line, but you might not need to; many cordless phones now have more than adequate ranges to cope with you taking the handset down the garden. If not, you can always buy a range extender (called a 'repeater'), which allows you to still receive calls dozens of metres away from the base unit. The same goes with Internet access. Why not create a wireless (WiFi) hotspot in your main house, which can then be accessed from your shed? The main factors in deciding how much it will all cost will be the distance of the shed away from the house and the location of all services.

HOW LARGE DOES THE SHED NEED TO BE?

It's a simple equation – your shed needs to be large enough for its purpose, while still remaining in keeping with your outside space. Planning rules may prevent you having an overlarge shed, but common sense also tells you not to make the structure out of proportion with your main house.

Don't compromise the garden as a whole. You have to weigh up the balance between having an adequately sized shed and keeping an appropriate amount of outside space. A drastic reduction in open or garden area can devalue a property, in spite of the extra floor space you've added.

How much space do you need for what you plan to do? Will one room suffice, or will you need partitions? Think about any furniture and equipment that you want to include. Don't forget storage space. If you are planning to use the room for an activity – especially a physical one such as exercise – ensure that there's adequate head height and width. Once you think you've worked out the size of the shed you'll need, plot it out in your garden. All you need is some wooden stakes or bamboo canes, and plenty of string. Only when you see the dimensions mapped out on the ground can you really get a sense of proportion and scale against your home and garden.

WHERE DO I SOURCE MY SHED?

You have a number of options. Pop down to any local hardware store or DIY outlet, and you will find a good selection of basic timber sheds on offer. These tend to be either small single-room larch lap sheds or small plastic garden 'tidies' or locker-style storage primarily designed for garden or tool storage, although some of the larger chains have widened their ranges to include playhouses, summer houses and other more person-friendly structures.

For something a bit more specialized, try one of the hundreds of shed companies that exist – there's a comprehensive directory at the back of this book. Depending on what you want, you'll find everything from self-build kits to designer dream sheds. What you choose will depend as much on your DIY skills as your budget, but most self-build kits are fairly straightforward for the average do-it-yourself buff. If you don't want to get your hands dirty, many of the larger shed manufacturers will gladly include delivery and installation as part of the quote. It's worth looking into this option – many of the larger sheds are far too complex to tackle yourself. Some manufacturers may actually insist that they erect the shed if you want a meaningful guarantee.

If money is no object, or you want something totally bespoke to your needs, most architects would be happy to offer their services on a shed project. A good architect will help you realize your ideas, and guide you, stress-free, through the planning and building process. Bear in mind, however, that good architects don't come cheap and will charge a fee that can either be based on a percentage of the total construction cost or on time expended, or as a total lump sum. Once a design is drawn up, a competent joiner can turn those ideas into reality and create something totally unique.

ORIENTATION AND WEATHER CONSIDERATIONS

If you have a choice about where your shed can go, give thought to its orientation. Do you need as much natural light as possible, or would a shady area be better? Does the shed need to be south-facing (or north-facing, if you live in the southern hemisphere), to make the most of the movement of the sun. If your plot is subject to adverse weather, find a sheltered spot away from prevailing wind and driving rain. Perhaps you want to make the most of the views and position your shed in an exposed part of the garden? In warmer climates, you may want to make the most of any outside seating area, such as a veranda or deck.

Do you want to see the house from your shed, or would you prefer to feel hidden from view? Many people overlook the concept of 'reverse views' – in other words, what you see from your back fence when you look back towards the house. This is a crucial part of the overall scheme and needs to be considered when looking at where to site the shed and how it relates to the main house.

Think about what you see from the windows of your shed – try to ensure the best views possible, making the most of the position of any existing trees, planting and other garden features. You'll also need to take into account any shade that the shed creates and adjust the planting accordingly. Laurels, bamboo, ivy, box, hostas, dogwood, hellebores, ferns and mahonias all like shady or partially shady conditions. A quick chat with your local garden centre will soon reveal the wide range of trees, shrubs and plants available that thrive in shade in your area. Sheds also make ideal candidates for trellising, allowing you to train any number of climbers and vines around the building.

Noise may be an issue if you plan to do a lot of entertaining in your shed. Landscaping can limit the amount of conversation and music that is transmitted over the garden fence to your neighbours.

Dense trees and hedges can go some way towards dampening the effect of noise, but walls and berms are a better option. Berms, or banks of soil, are often used by landscape gardeners to deaden the effect of noise, either from traffic or neighbouring properties. If your garden already has a naturally undulating terrain, build the shed in the bottom of any dip, where noisy will be less likely to carry and your shed will fit neatly.

Even water features can help to reduce noise pollution, as the sound of running water can mask a certain amount of low-level noise. Fountains and similar water features, or even a pond, will add a sense of calm and relaxation to your outdoor space too.

DEALING WITH TREES

In the planning stages of your shed, you'll need to check that the construction of your shed isn't going to affect any trees protected by preservation orders. Preservation orders make it an offence to cut down, uproot or destroy any protected tree(s) without first having obtained permission from your local council. All types of tree can be protected, whether as single trees or as part of a woodland or stand of trees, so always check before you start merrily chopping away.

You may also need to trim back any overhanging branches from your neighbour's trees – rules vary, but in most cases you have the right to trim any encroaching branches from a neighbour's tree, but only back to your boundary. The same applies to tree roots. Entering someone's property without permission to cut a tree is illegal. If your neighbour won't cooperate and you think that the tree may damage your new shed, talk to your local authority. If a neighbour refuses to tackle a dangerous tree that affects your property, you may be able to get a court injunction to have it removed.

PLANNING ACCESS

Even if your shed is going to be an integral part of your garden, it's still vital to think about creating a viable access track, whether it's a boardwalk or gravel path. Rain will soon turn your lawn into a slipping hazard; if you plan to use your shed on a regular basis, you'll need to make the route from home to shed a safe one. Equally, if you live in a dry climate, you don't want your path to turn into a dusty track. Remove any obstacles along your pathway, especially if you're

going to be carrying goods to and from your shed, and keep the pathway clear at all times. Wooden steps and decking can soon become slippery, thanks to green algae, so always use non-slip wooden boards or apply an anti-slip finish to any timber.

If anybody who will be using the shed has mobility problems, it's important to address those at the planning and design stage. Footpaths of a width of 1800mm (preferably 2000mm) will allow wheelchairs and prams to pass. Footpaths should also be firm, with defined edges and no overhanging objects. You'll also need to think about installing ramps with a gentle gradient, and doorways should be wide enough to accommodate any mobility aids, such as a wheelchair or walker.

That said, just because the access has to be practical and safe, doesn't

mean that it can't be an integral part of the design. If the shed is hidden at the end of the garden, could the pathway wind its way gently down the plot, taking you on a relaxed tour along the way?

DO I NEED PLANNING PERMISSION?

The good news is that some sheds don't need planning permission. Depending on where you live, however, there are a number of exceptions to the rule, and several variables apply relating to height, size and the shed's intended use.

Planning authorities tend to want permission if you live in an area of special interest (historical or environmental) or if you want to build a shed that is especially big or closer to a highway than the original house. They will also want to know if you plan to use the shed for non-domestic purposes, such as. parking a commercial vehicle or running a business. Don't panic if you want to work from home. Most planning authorities don't view a home office in the same light as other businesses.

The planners may ask some simple questions: has your home become business premises first and a home second? Will your business lead to increased traffic or parking in a residential area? Does your business involve any unusual activities for a residential area or activities that may disturb your neighbours at unreasonable hours or create other forms of nuisance, such as noise or smells? Do you have customers or visitors coming to your home business on a regular basis? If you can answer no to these questions, there's a good chance that the planning authorities won't have a problem with you working from your shed.

That said, the rules vary region to region, country to country, so it's absolutely essential that you contact your local planning department before you start work, even if you think your shed won't require planning. Building regulations may also come into play if you are constructing an especially large shed, installing services or planning to turn the shed into a sleeping space. They'll also want to know if your shed is going to have two storeys. Again, contact your local planning department to find out whether you need to comply with any specific legal requirements.

NEIGHBOURS AND BOUNDARY ISSUES

On a final note, it's worth saying a few things about neighbours and boundaries. At the design stage, you'll need to consider planning issues such as overshadowing and noise, and practical issues such as shed maintenance, if you want to build close to a boundary. Talk to the planning department – there may be covenants or local by-laws that you have to consider.

Contrary to popular opinion, not everyone has a 'right to light', but it is something to consider if you are planning to erect a shed close to your neighbour's boundary. In the UK, for example, it is possible to earn a 'right to light', but you need to prove you've had a minimum of 20 years of uninterrupted light to a building, generally through a window or door. Above all, it's important to be neighbourly – everyone has the right to use their property as they please, as long as they in turn don't interfere unreasonably with other people's enjoyment of their property. Be considerate about where and how the shed will be used, and you shouldn't run into any problems with those who live around you.

BUILDING AND LOOKING AFTER YOUR SHED

Now that you've worked out what you are going to build, it's time to tackle how you're going to put that into practice. Most shed companies will be happy to talk you through the building process, or erect the structure for you. Depending on the complexity of your shed, here's a quick list of some of the practical building considerations to bear in mind:

Materials Timber is the most popular construction material for sheds. Your shed designer can give you advice on different types of hardwood and any treatment that they require in order to create a sturdy, long-lasting, sustainable shed. Cedar and pine are popular choices for garden sheds, while self-cleaning and insulated glass, steel, tin and sometimes concrete can also be used.

The great advantage of wood is that it can be extended outside the shed to provide visual continuity in the form of decking, verandas, balustrades, window boxes and shutters, in keeping with the appealing nature of a garden structure that provides a sense of escape and mystery.

Foundations Sheds require foundations for two main reasons. First, being made of timber, most sheds will rot if placed directly onto a soil surface. Foundations keep the building nice and dry, either by raising it above ground level or providing an impermeable barrier between the soil and the shed base. Sheds also need foundations to keep them stable. The right foundations will level an uneven site and provide a solid, square base on which the shed can sit.

There are no hard-and-fast rules about the type of foundations you will need. Small sheds, typically those used for storage, usually don't need much in the way of foundations. Some properly levelled paving slabs or concrete padstones, placed strategically, to raise the shed off the ground and provide a level surface, should suffice. Some people use railway sleepers or timber blocks; however, over time, these carry moisture from the ground into the shed.

For larger sheds, there is a number of different foundation types to consider, depending on manufacturers' recommendations and the type of site on which you plan to put the shed. Some sheds will sit happily on a traditional solid concrete base or concrete strip foundations, while others have 'metal shoes' that sit on concrete padstones set into the ground. (The number of shoes and pads varies with the size of the building.) Some sheds also come with their own steel or timber chassis, which removes the need for foundations entirely.

As a general rule, your shed's manufacturer will have specific guidelines about the depth and type of foundations needed. If you are erecting a very large shed, a surveyor may want to check on the site's suitability for the intended building. Ground composition, trees, drainage, geological faults and past mining can all have an effect on the type of foundations required. Above all, don't scrimp on foundations. Poor footings shorten the building's life and could make it hazardous to use in the long run.

Insulation If you plan to use your shed all year round, it's important to give some thought to insulation.

Good insulation will keep your shed warm in winter, but will also help to maintain a comfortable, cool temperature during the summer months. It'll save you money in the long run – poorly insulated buildings are expensive to heat and expensive to cool, and increase your carbon footprint.

The timber walls of a shed lend themselves to internal insulation, so the task is fairly straightforward and relatively inexpensive. Without getting too technical, there are two main types of internal wall insulation. The first is a type of thermal plasterboard that is backed with an insulating material (usually up to 90mm thick). The boards are fitted directly to the timber battens inside your shed; the thicker the board, the warmer

(or cooler in the hotter months) the insulation. Sheds also lend themselves to the second form of internal insulation – filling the spaces between the battens with insulation, then covering over with plasterboard, plywood or tongue-and-groove cladding. As with all things, you get what you pay for – decent insulation will make your shed eminently more usable and enjoyable, and expand its range of possible uses. Good-quality insulation also reduces the transmission of noise into and out of your shed. Some of the more expensive sheds will come with insulation already fitted, or as an integral part of the structure.

Dealing with damp One of the biggest challenges with sheds is dealing with damp. To prevent rising damp (damp coming up from the ground), there are various options. If the shed sits on concrete blocks, you'll need to put a damp-proof membrane (DPM) between the blocks and the timber joists, to prevent the timber rotting. One of the good things about sheds that sit on blocks is that they tend to allow a good flow of air to circulate underneath, naturally encouraging the building to stay dry. Solid concrete floors will also need to incorporate a DPM. Some sheds come with a damp-proof membrane already sandwiched in the timber floor, so you'll need to check with the manufacturer before work starts.

To help the shed walls resist damp, you can also put a vapour barrier on the warm side of the insulation (i.e. the internal face of the wall insulation). The only problem with many damp-proofing measures is that they tend to trap water inside the shed, causing

condensation. Look into breathable damp-proof systems that allow condensation out without letting water back in.

Heating While it's more than possible to have central heating in a large shed (it'll need its own boiler and access to a fuel supply), most sheddies won't want, or need, to install an entire new system. Depending on what you use your shed for, you may need different sorts of heating. If you plan to spend long periods working or sitting, you'll probably want some kind of system that provides a pleasant background heat – slim-line convection heaters, halogen heaters or oil-filled radiators are three possible options, all of which will need access to electrical power points. If you use your shed only sporadically, fan heaters and ceramic heaters can provide fast,

instant heat, but usually cost more to run. If you don't need any specific type of heating in your shed, but are worried about burst pipes over the winter months or damage from mildew, you can buy 'frost watcher' heaters for sheds, which keep the temperature just above freezing.

If you don't have an electricity supply running to your shed, wood-burning stoves have proved a popular and economical choice with many shed owners. They're relatively eco-friendly if they burn efficiently, and they make a wonderful focal point to crowd around on a chilly evening. Just remember that you'll need to factor a flue pipe into your shed design, and think about fire safety implications. Another option for sheds without power is a portable gas or oil heater, both of which are inexpensive and readily available.

Electricity Any electricity supply to your shed will need to run from the mains unit in your home. Getting electricity to the bottom of your garden is actually a fairly straightforward task, but it's imperative that you have the work carried out by a properly qualified electrician. Outdoor electrics have the potentially to be lethal, thanks to the combination of water and electricity, so you'll need to make sure that any works comply with wiring and building regulations. You may even have to notify your local authority about the intended work, depending on the complexity and location of the new wires. Always check before work starts.

When you are planning your shed, think about where the plug sockets and light switches will go. You'll also need to consider the lighting itself. Do you need specific task lighting or more general overhead lighting? Would the shed benefit from outside lights, and what about lighting the pathway from shed to main house, especially if you want to use it after dark? Will any of the equipment you are using in the shed need a power supply? Remember to factor in any computer equipment, telephones and security systems. Talk to the electrician about your plans for the building – he or she will need to design a system which can cope with the extra demand.

Water supplies and waste It can be a real hassle having to go back to the main house every time you need to use the bathroom or want to make a cup of tea or coffee. The easiest way to get both hot and cold water to your shed is to run a basic cold-water supply from the main house, then use an on-demand electric water heater to convert the cold water to hot. (You could run a hot-water supply from the main house, but it tends to lose heat if it has to travel any distance.) An on-demand water heater will provide enough hot water for hand-washing facilities; however, if you want to include a shower, the best option is to install an electric model that also heats the water as you use it. Dishwashers and washing machines both tend to heat their own water, so a cold-water supply will also be more than adequate for a laundry/utility shed.

Once you have dealt with the water supply to your shed, you need to think about where it's going to go afterwards. 'Grey water' (waste water generated from dish washing, laundry and bathing) needs different treatment than 'black water' (from the toilet). A soakaway may be all you need if you plan to discharge only a small amount of grey water from your shed, but large amounts of grey water and any amount at all of black water will need to go into a mains drain or septic tank.

Mains drains tend to be located next to houses, so you might need a pump to push waste water from the shed back up the garden, especially if the waste water has to climb any kind of gradient. In all cases, talk to the building control officer at your local authority – he or she will be able to tell you what system is necessary for your shed.

Paints and finishes Exterior timber is subject to a great number of stresses – whichever finish you choose will need to be water-repellent and resistant to fading from the elements. It will also ideally protect your shed from the sun's harmful UV rays. As the building will be in your back

garden, any paint or varnish used should ideally also be harmless to pets and plants.

Certain timber, such as oak, can be left untreated if you prefer, or your shed may come pre-finished, but if you are painting it yourself you can choose from any number of options, from subtle wood stains to bright gloss paints. Much will depend on the type and surface texture of the timber; however, if you are able to opt for an eco-friendly option, then so much the better. Wood finishes, including paints, stains and varnishes, often contain high levels of volatile organic compounds (VOCs), which are known to cause air pollution and have been linked to health problems such as allergies and breathing difficulties. When you are choosing a wood finish, select one with the best eco credentials

you can find. If possible, look for 'natural' paints or finishes with low or no VOC content.

If you are stripping paint from a shed, it's also important to take care. Pre-1950s paint often contained lead, which is very dangerous if inhaled or ingested. If you suspect that you are dealing with lead paint, you need to take extreme care, especially around children and pregnant women. Most local councils have advice leaflets about dealing with lead paint, but you can also find helpful information at websites for organizations such as the UK's DEFRA (www.defra.gov.uk).

Security Unfortunately, sheds can be a target for thieves. If you are planning to keep anything of value in the shed, it's important to include security measures in your costings. Depending on how secure your shed needs to be you can choose anything from simple padlocks to state-of-the-art CCTV. The reality is, however, that any security measures will only be as good as the build quality of the shed – a determined burglar can easily prise open a flimsy door or window. The best advice is to choose a sturdy, well-built shed, and make sure that all the doors and windows have adequate locks.

Install a shed alarm, and display a notice stating that the premises are alarmed. A security light is also a good idea – it helps you to see your shed from the house and deters any potential criminals from approaching. Police often advise having a gravel path around the shed – burglars don't like these because they make a noise when anyone is walking on them.

Keep valuables out of view, if possible, either by closing the curtains or blinds when you are not using the shed, or by locking any valuables away when not in use. It's also essential to add up the value of the contents of your shed, for insurance purposes. Despite their having computers, TVs and other expensive equipment inside, many sheds are left unlocked, and, worse, many are uninsured. Check your household insurance policy to ensure that the value of things stored inside is covered by your contents policy. Many household policies cover 'occasional' working from home (called teleworking), but have restrictions on equipment that is specifically owned by your business. If necessary, extend your cover so that there are no 'holes' in the policy you may later regret.

Maintenance Like any other building, sheds need ongoing maintenance if they are going to last any length of time. Wood expands and contracts with the weather conditions, so timber sheds need sprucing up every few years, whether it's reapplying wood preservative or sloshing on a new coat of paint. Whichever finish you choose, the key to a successful job will be preparation. You may have to scrape off loose paint, fill holes, clean, sand or prime any surfaces before applying a new coat. Always follow the manufacturer's guidelines.

Timber's worst enemy is damp. Any areas of rotten wood should be replaced as soon as you discover them, but you should also try to establish what's causing the problem. Blocked gutters, a failed damp-proof course, a leaky roof or badly fitting window/door frames are common culprits. Do a quick check before making repairs, and fix the underlying problem as well.

UK SOURCES

BESPOKE SHEDS

Artisan Shepherds Huts
The Granary
Grange Farm
Lindfield
West Sussex
RH16 2QY
Tel: 01444 400183
www.artisan-shepherdshuts.co.uk

Blueforest Treehouse
1 Bensfield Farm Cottages
Best Beech
Wadhurst
East Sussex
TN5 6JR, UK
Tel: 01892 750090
www.blueforest.com
Treehouses and ecolodges

Border Oak
Kingsland Sawmills
Kingsland
Leominster
Herefordshire, HR6 9S
Tel: 01568 708752
www.borderoak.com
Bespoke oak structures i

Breeze House
Sunnyhills Road
Barnfields
Leek
Staffordshire
ST13 5RJ
Tel: 01538 398488
www.breezehouse.co.uk
High-quality Colonial-style wooden
garden gazebos

Cheeky Monkey Treehouses
Tel: 01403 732452
www.cheekymonkeytreehouses.co.uk

The Children's Cottage Co.
Tel: 01363 772061
www.play-houses.com

Cock-a-Hoop
Bignor, Nr Pulborough
West Sussex
RH20 1PQ
Tel: 01798 869919
E-mail: info@gdtimberdesigns.co.uk
www.gdtimberdesigns.co.uk
Bespoke children's structures

Courtyard Designs
Hollywall Farm
Stoke Prior
Leominster
Herefordshire
HR6 0NF
Tel: 01568 760540
www.courtyarddesigns.co.uk
Makers of high-quality traditionally
styled timber outbuildings

Ecospace
3 Illiffe Yard
Kennington
London
SE17 3QA
Tel: 020 7703 4004
E-mail: info@ecospacestudios.com
www.ecospacestudios.com
Eco-friendly green-roofed studios

English Heritage Buildings
Woods Corner
East Sussex
TN21 9LQ
Tel: 001424 838643
www.ehbp.com

Flyte So Fancy
The Cottage
Pulham
Dorchester
Dorset DT2 7DX
Tel: 01300 345229
www.flytesofancy.co.uk
Hand-built poultry and pet sheds

Flights of Fantasy
Mill Farm
Congham
King's Lynn
Norfolk
PE32 1DP
Tel: 01485 600809
www.flightsoffantasy.co.uk
Craftsmen and designers of high-quality
children's playhouses

GD Timber Designs
Stone Cottages
Bignor
Nr Pulborough
West Sussex
RH20 1PQ
Tel: 01798 869919
www.gdtimberdesigns.co.uk

The Garden House Limited
The Barn
Manston Green Industries
Preston Road
Manston
Kent CT12 5BA
Tel: 01843 821851
www.thegardenhouse.ltd.uk

Garden Lodges
Tel: 0800 0434821
www.gardenlodges.co.uk
Range of contemporary garden
buildings from offices to studios and
large suites

Green Building Store
Heath House Mill
Heath House Lane
Bolster Moor
West Yorkshire HD7 4JW
Tel: 01484 461705
www.greenbuildingstore.co.uk
Eco building products

Homelodge
Kingswell Point
Crawley
Winchester
Hampshire SO21 2PU
Tel: (01962) 881480
www.homelodge.co.uk
High-quality modular timber buildings,
including home offices

The Home Office Company
TempleCo Ten Limited
Stonestile Barn
Harthill
Charing
Kent TN27 OHW
Tel: 01233 712710
www.tc10.com

Hut Design
Unit 8b
Canford Business park
Magna Road
Wimborne
Dorset BH21 3BT
Tel: 01202 574 584

MPB Garden Buildings
Coppice Gate
Lye Head
Bewley
Worcester DY12 2UX
Tel: 01299 266000
www.themalverncollection.co.uk
Manufacturers and installers of the
Malvern Collection, a cottage range of
garden rooms

Norwegian Log Buildings
230 London Road
Reading
RG6 1AH
Tel: 0118 966 9236
Fax: 0118 966 0456
www.norwegianlog.co.uk
Solid log cabins, lodges and other
garden buildings

Pure Folly
Tel: 07802 482638
Email: info@purefolly.com
www.purefolly.com
Bespoke garden structures, including
Gothic ruins, grottoes, towers and
driftwood gazebos

Rooms Outdoor
Studio 3B
Clapham North Art Centre
26-32 Voltaire Road
London
SW4 6DH
Tel: 020 8332 3022
www.roomsoutdoor.co.uk
Bespoke garden offices

Scotts of Thrapston
Bridge Street
Thrapston
Northamptonshire
NN14 4LR
England
Tel: (01832) 732366
Website: www.scottsofthrapston.co.uk

Squirrel Design
The Old Cake House
The Dairy
Pinkney Park
Malmesbury
Wiltshire SN16 0NX
Tel: 01666 840703
www.squirreldesign.co.uk
Handcrafted tree houses and retreats

The Garden Escape
Up Beyond
Wye View Lane
Symonds Yat West
Herefordshire HR9 6BN
Tel: 0870 2427024
www.thegardenescape.co.uk
Contemporary garden buildings

The Gypsy Caravan Company
Garboldisham
Norfolk
IP22 2RJ
Tel: 01953 681995
www.gypsycaravancompany.co.uk
Hand-built gypsy caravans and
wagon restoration

The Private House
Pusey
Nr. Faringdon
Oxon SN7 8QB
Tel: 01367 870 582
Email: design@theprivatehouse.com
www.theprivatehouse.com
Makers of exclusive 'Retreats', custom-
built showman's caravans

The Qube
Tel: 01604 785786
www.theqube.co.uk
Contemporary garden offices

Taylors Garden Buildings
www.taylorsgardenbuildings.co.uk
Huge range of simple sheds, potting
sheds, summer houses, log cabins,
playhouses and greenhouses

Treehouse Guides
www.treehouseguides.com
DIY instructions and diagrams for tree
houses available to download

Wormersleys
Tel: 01924 400651
www.womersleys.co.uk
Natural insulation and eco
building materials

OFF-THE-SHELF SHEDS

B&Q
www.diy.com
DIY superstore with off-the-shelf sheds
and garden tidies

Buy Sheds Direct
www.buyshedsdirect.co.uk
Tel: 0844 248 9824

Homebase
Tel: 0845 077 8888
www.homebase.co.uk

Notcutts
Notcutts Garden Centres
Woodbridge
Suffolk
IP12 4AF
Tel: 01394 383344
www.notcutts.co.uk

Wyevale Garden Centres Ltd
258 Bath Road
Slough
Berkshire
SL1 4DX
Tel: 0844 800 8082

ARCHITECTS

Anderson Mason Dale
1615 Seventeenth Street
Denver CO 80202
USA
Tel: +1 303 294 9448
www.amdarchitects.com

Square Feet Architects Ltd
10 Perrins Court
London
NW3 1QS
Tel: 020 7431 4500

Todd Oldham
Tel: +1 212 226 4668
www.toddoldham.com

FURNITURE AND FURNISHINGS

Habitat
www.habitat.co.uk
Furniture and soft urnishings,
including home office equipment
and stylish storage

IKEA
www.ikea.com
Furniture and furnishings including
home office and garden

WEBSITES AND BLOGS

Reader's Sheds
www.readersheds.co.uk
Shed enthusiasts website with
comprehensive directory of suppliers
and shed blog

SALVO
www.salvo.co.uk
A large directory of suppliers of
architectural salvage, including sheds
and garden buildings

Sheds Heaven
www.sheds-heaven.co.uk
Comprehensive directory of garden
building suppliers in the UK

Shedworking
www.shedworking.co.uk
Publishers of *The Shed* magazine and
on-line lifestyle guide for 'sheddies'

AUSTRALIA SOURCES

Aarons Outdoor Creations
59 Radford Rd
Reservoir VIC 3073
Tel: +61 1300 305 325
www.aaronsoutdoor.com.au
Timber garden buildings, cabins and
pet sheds

All About Sheds
236 Princes Highway
South Nowra NSW 2541
Tel: +61 (0)2 4422 5033
E-mail: info@allaboutsheds.com.au
www.allaboutsheds.com.au
Wide range of garden sheds, animal
sheds and storage sheds

Australian Summerhouse Company
244 New Line Road
Dural NSW 2158
Tel: +61 (0)2 9651 4840
E-mail: mail@summerhouse.net.au
Summer houses and gazebos

Blue Mountain Yurts
Tel: +61 (0)405 072 616
E-mail: info@bluemountain.yurts.com
www.bluemountainyurts.com
Contemporary yurts for your garden

Brisbane Garden Sheds
210 Beatty Road
Archerfield QLD 4108
Tel: +61 (0)7 3277 3008
www.brisbanegardensheds.com.au
Wide range of utility sheds

Canberra Outdoor Structures
143 Gilmore Road
Queanbeyan NSW 2620
Tel: +61 (0)2 6299 6735
www.canberraoutdoorstructures.com.au
Garden sheds, studios, cabins and
playhouses

Cubby House
Unit 1, 2 Turbo Road
Kings Park NSW 2149
Tel: +61 (0)2 9679 7977
E-mail: sales@cubbyhouse.com.au
www.cubbyhouse.com.au
Western cedar children's cubbyhouses

eHabitat
Lvl 2, 49 Rooke St Mall
Devonport TAS 7310
Tel: +61 (0)3 6248 8644
Prefabricated eco-friendly contemporary
garden buildings

Glasshouse Country Enterprises
Cnr Glasshouse Mountain Road &
Back Creek Road
Beerwah QLD 4519
Tel: +61 (0)7 5494 0933
E-mail: cubbies@gce.com.au
www.gce.com.au
Cubbyhouses, forts, sheds and cabins

Greenwood Garden Products
PO Box 315
Mona Vale NSW 1660
Tel: +61 (0)2 9999 5970
E-mail: sales@greenwood
gardenproducts.com
www.greenwoodgarden
products.com.au
Custom-made granny flats, weekenders,
home offices, backyard cabins, studios
and teenage retreats

Home and Garden Storage
www.homeandgardenstorage.com.au
Portal for everything to do with garden
sheds, including shed dealers

Modabode
Factory 3, 89 North Street
Albury NSW 2640
Tel: +61 (0)2 6021 8877
E-mail: ebode@mod-eco.com.au
Architectural modular garden studios
and annexes

Noek Design
E-mail: info@neokdesign.com
www.neokdesign.com
Architect-designed Zen-like deckhouses

Prebuilt
219 Colchester Road
Kilsyth VIC 3137
Tel: +61 (0)3 9761 5544
info@prebuilt.com.au
Eco-friendly kit homes, including pods
and retreats

Shady Characters
1/59 Randolph St
Rocklea QLD 4106
Tel: +61 (0)7 3275 1300
E-mail: sheds@shadycharacters.com.au
Portable and permanent outdoor
structures

Shed Strong
Head Office
18 Gore Street
Cambooya QLD 4358
E-mail: info@shedstrong.com.au
Tel: +61 1800 131 000
Pre-engineered steel sheds, including
workshops, granny flats, studios and
boat sheds

Smartshax
Upton Building Pty Ltd.
PO Box 272
Avalon Beach NSW 2107
E-mail: uptonbuilding@bigpond.com
www.smartshax.com.au
Lightweight, eco-friendly
contemporary huts

TS1
Suite 330/197 Bourke St
MELBOURNE VIC 3000
Tel: +61 (0)3 9662 3223
info@ts1now.com.au
www.ts1now.com.au
Ultra-modern architecturally designed
pop-up garden rooms

PICTURE CREDITS

1 Country Living/Simon Bevan: 2 Jacqui Small Publishing/Frédéric Vasseur/Rachel Parnaby's home in London; 3 Country Living/Simon Bevan; 4–5 Rebecca Duke/designer Bill Amberg; 6 Philippe Perdereau; 7 Marianne Majerus/design John Sarbutt; 8 Undine Pröhl; 9 Country Living/Bob Smith; 10–11 Country Living/Alex Ramsay; 11 Country Living/Kate Gadsby; 12–13 Marianne Majerus/The Merrill Lynch Garden, RHS Chelsea Flower Show 2005, design Andy Sturgeon; 14 Country Living/Simon Bevan; 15 Country Living/Catherine Gratwicke; 16 Country Living/Simon Bevan; 17 above Harpur Garden Images/Jerry Harpur/design and owned by Cary Wolinsky Norwell, Mass USA; 17 below Photozest/Inside; 18 above Scotts of Thrapston Limited; 18 below Jacqui Small Publishing/Frédéric Vasseur/Nina Gustafsson's Swedish home; 19 IPC + Syndication/Homes & Gardens; 20 Photozest/Inside/S Clement/stylist C Mamet; 21 Philippe Perdereau; 22 below The Garden Escape; 22–23 View Pictures/Kilian O'Sullivan/Ullmayer Sylvester Architects; 23 below left The Modern Shed Company; 23 below right The Modern Shed Company; 24 View Pictures/Kilian O'Sullivan/Ullmayer Sylvester Architects; 25 Mark Gandy, designed by Kim Parker; 26 View Pictures/Kilian O'Sullivan/Ullmayer Sylvester Architects; 27 Camera Press/ACP/Simon Griffiths/Christian Jenkins Design www.cjdesign.com.au; 28 Ecospace/Andy Spain; 29 Jacqui Small Publishing/Simon Upton/a mountain retreat in Colorado, designed by Ron Mason; 30 Camera Press/ACP/Valerie Martin; 31 above Redcover.com/Winfried Heinze; 31 below Photozest/Inside/T Jeanson; 32 above left Christian Sarramon; 32 above right Country Living/Simon Bevan; 32 below Photozest/Inside/Solvi dos Santos; 33 Taverne-Agency/Nathalie Krag; 34 above left Marianne Majerus/design Bunny Guinness; 34 above centre The Gypsy Caravan Company; 34 above right Philippe Perdereau; 34 below Country Living; 35 Narratives/Claire Richardson; 36–37 Jacqui Small Publishing/Frédéric Vasseur/Janine Hosegood's home in London; 38 Ecospace/Andy Spain; 39 Jacqui Small Publishing/Alexander James/Ailsa Barry & Jonathan Sakula's London garden studio designed by The Garden Escape; 40–41 IPC + Syndication/Ideal Home/Dan Duchars; 42 Redcover.com/Patrick Spense; 43 Homelodge Buildings Limited; 44 Redcover.com/Winfried Heinze; 45 Ecospace/George Logan; 46 IPC + Syndication/Homes & Gardens/Jan Baldwin; 47 above & below right IPC + Syndication/LivingEtc./Nick Allen; 47 below left IPC + Syndication/Homes & Gardens/Jan Baldwin; 48–55 Ecospace/Andy Spain; 56 Country Living/James Merrell; 56–57 Country Living/Nial McDiarmid; 57 IPC + Syndication/Country Homes & Interiors/Tim Young; 58 Country Living/Simon Bevan; 59 Photozest/Inside/Ivan Terestchencko; 60 left Country Living/Caroline Arber; 60 centre Country Living; 60 right Marianne Majerus/design Sally Brampton; 61 Country Living/Caroline Arber; 62 IPC + Syndication/Country Homes & Interiors/Tom Leighton; 63 Country Living/Simon Bevan; 64 Country Living/Charlie Colmer; 65 Artisan Shepherd's Huts; 66 Country Living/Simon Brown; 67 Country Living/Simon Bevan; 68 above Narratives/Jan Baldwin/designed by Annabel Lewis of VV Rouleaux; 68 below left IPC + Syndication/Country Homes & Interiors/Tim Young; 68 below right Marianne Majerus/design Mary Nuttall; 69 Country Living/Catherine Gratwicke; 70–73 Jacqui Small Publishing/Alexander James/Linda Barker's London shed; 74–75 IPC + Syndication/LivingEtc./Nick Allen; 76–77 Jacqui Small Publishing/Alexander James/Malcolm Temple's London shed; 78 Harpur Garden Images/Jerry Harpur/design John & Kathleen Holmes, CA, USA; 78–79 Gap Photos/John Glover/design Karen Maskell; 79 Philippe Perdereau/ Hampton Court Flower Show/Southend-on-Sea Borough Council; 80 IPC + Syndication/House & Gardens/Caroline Arber; 81 Country Living/Kate Gadsby; 82 Gap Photos/Helen Edwards/design Claire Potter; 83 above Country Living/ James Robinson; 83 below Mainstreamimages/Ray Main/www.re-foundobjects.com; 84 IPC + Syndication/Ideal Home/Alun Callender; 85 above IPC + Syndication/Essentials/Jo Tyler; 85 below Photozest/Inside/S Clement/stylist C Mamet; 86 Photozest/Inside/Solvi dos Santos; 87 Photozest/Inside/S Clement/stylist C Mamet; 88 Country Living/Simon Bevan; 89 above left IPC + Syndication/Country Homes & Interiors/Tom Leighton; 89 above right IPC + Syndication/Homes & Gardens/Caroline Arber; 89 below Country Living/Simon Bevan; 90 above left Harpur Garden Images/Marcus Harpur/design Maryanne Nicholls, Suffolk; 90 above right Photozest/Inside/L Waumann; 90 below Photozest/Inside/L Waumann; 91 Country Living/James Merrell; 92 Photozest/Inside/Ivan Terestchenko; 93 Gettyimages/Christopher Drake/Red Cover; 94 left Photozest/Inside/S Clement/stylist C Mamet; 94 right Philippe Perdereau; 95 Country Living/Alex Ramsay; 96 Andreas von Einsiedel; 97 above Redcover.com/Brian Harrison; 97 below Taverne-Agency/Dennis Brandsma; 98 left Derek St Romaine; 98 right Redcover.com/Practical Pictures; 99 Philippe Perdereau/Jardin d'Anne-Marie; 100 Photozest/Inside; 101 Philippe Perdereau; 102 Camera Press/Maison/Michael Fernin; 103 Andreas von Einsiedel, design by La Cabane Perchée; 104–105 Country Living/Simon Bevan; 106 Taverne-Agency/Nathalie Krag; 107 Taverne-Agency/John Dummer; 108 Photozest/Inside/Ingalill Snitt; 109 Photozest/Inside/J Hall; 110–111 IPC + Syndication/Country Homes & Interiors/Tom Leighton; 112 Andrea Jones/design by Maureen Busby; 113 above left Photozest/Inside; 113 above right Photozest/Inside; 113 below Artisan Shepherd's Huts; 114–119 Camera Press/Côté Sud/Nicolas Matheus; 120–123 Country Living/Jamie Long; 124–127 Camera Press/ Côté Sud /Bernard Touillon; 128–129 Camera Press/Marie Claire Maison/José Postic; 130 Narratives/Emma Lee; 131 Country Living/Tara Fisher; 132 Photozest/Inside/K Damstedt; 133 left Redcover.com/Alun Callender; 133 right Redcover.com/Andrew Twort; 134–135 Jacqui Small Publishing/Simon Upton/Tricia Foley's home on Long Island, tableware by Wedgwood; 136 Camera Press/Avantages/Christophe Valentin; 137 Camera Press/Maison/Camille Stoos; 138–141 Redcover.com/Christopher Drake/www.cabbagesandroses.com; 142–145 Jacqui Small Publishing/Alexander James/Sean Latus's shed designed by Square Feet Architects; 146–147 The Private House/Andrew Twort; 148–149 Andreas von Einsiedel, fabric designer Sue Timney; 150–151 Photozest/Inside/Ingalill Snitt; 152 Country Living/Simon Bevan; 153 Photozest/Inside; 154–155 Jacqui Small Publishing/Simon Upton/a mountain retreat in Colorado, designed by Ron Mason; 156–157 Camera Press/Maison Française/Christine Soler/Aude de la Conté; 158 above left Ecospace/Andy Spain; 158 above right Camera Press/Maison Française/Nicolas Matheus; 158 below Ecospace/Andy Spain; 159 Photozest/Inside/Ingalill Snitt; 160–163 Mainstream-images/Paul Raeside/The Private House; 164–167 Richard Powers/designer Todd Oldham; 168–169 Photozest/Inside/HoP/Toresdotter; 170 Marianne Majerus/Elton Hall, Herefordshire; 170–171 Redcover.com/Johnny Bouchier; 171 Marianne Majerus/design Ben Wilson; 172 IPC + Syndication/LivingEtc./Paul Massey; 173 Country Living/Simon Bevan; 174 above left Redcover.com/Simon McBride; 174 above right Flights of Fantasy; 174 below The Gypsy Caravan Company; 175 above Redcover.com/Chris Tubbs; 175 below Flights of Fantasy; 176 above The Private House/Andrew Twort; 176 below The Gypsy Caravan Company; 177 The Private House/Andrew Twort; 178 Camera Press/Côté Ouest/Ingalill Snitt; 179 Jacqui Small Publishing/Frédéric Vasseur/David Berg's house in Sweden; 180–183 Camera Press/Maison Française/Christophe Dugied/Isabelle Creiser; 184–185 Jacqui Small Publishing/Alexander James/Malcolm Temple's London shed; 186 The Modern Shed Company; 187 The Garden Escape; front endpaper: Mark Gandy, designed by Kim Parker; back endpaper: Country Living/Caroline Arber

AUTHOR'S ACKNOWLEDGEMENTS

Thanks to everyone at Jacqui Small, especially Jo, Nadine, Sarah and, of course, Jacqui; thank you for asking me to write the book in the first place and for making it so beautiful and readable. Thanks also to Lisa Sykes at Country Living magazine for putting in a good word – I owe you one. My thanks to all the real life 'sheddies' featured throughout the book – the case studies are what bring the book alive, and my sincere gratitude goes to everyone who was brave enough to let us poke around in their back garden. And, finally, thank you to my family for being endlessly supportive.

This book is dedicated to Nicola and Tom – congratulations, and about time too.